# NOT FORGETTING

## *A Mad Child's Tale*

*This is a memoir. The events and conversations in this book have been set down to the best of the author's ability, although some names and details have been changed to protect the privacy of individuals.*

*ISBN 978-1-7929-5576-1*

# *NOT FORGETTING*

## *A Mad Child's Tale*

LIZ DYER

*To my grandmother*

Violet Annie SOAL

*Cook and comforter*

# Preface

This tale grew in the telling, as an earlier author once wrote. A greater author than I: but Tolkien wrote fantasy and expressed beauty, pain and struggle through his imagined world. I cannot do that.

I must write as history, as my own story threads its way through the lives of others, and the heddles of time clack up and down weaving us into the 'fabric of society' with all its snags and moth-holes and broken ends, and its intricate glittering brocades.

In 1996, after decades of separation from my family I was given two archives of papers; the contents of three brief-cases and ten parcels from Don Steel of the Society of Genealogists, and from another source, an entire car-load of private memorabilia hoarded by my mother.

My husband Neil spent the last seven years of his life helping me sort and identify this material including Ration Books, ID cards, school reports, personal notes and photo albums (one of them forged!) We tracked down relatives who made sense of my life at last. I promised Neil before he died, that I would continue, and eventually write my story. It has taken another fifteen years.

I have kept notes and diaries all my life, the earliest dictated to my father in the days before I could write. Over the years they have been mislaid, rediscovered, forgotten, remembered, and repeatedly transcribed and condensed to save space, and remove the tedious and self-pitying elements. In 2015 I combined them with my other material, set all in chronological order and started writing.

I aimed for 250 words a day for a year, posting them as a series of anecdotes on social media. I reached the last file three years later at a much larger word count, and with requests that I publish a series of memoirs. This is the first.

*Liz Dyer*
*3rd January 2019*

# *Prologue: . . .*

***BIRMINGHAM***

**Charles Innes**
My grandfather. Founder and owner of Purus Bakeries
**Edith Innes, nee Manning**
My grandmother. A matriarch. Stern but kind

**Charles Henry Davies Innes**
My Uncle Harry. Master Baker. Tall, strong eldest son
**Rosa, nee Wood**
His wife. Plump and warm.
**Patricia**
Their daughter. My afflicted cousin Pat

**Wilfred Gordon Innes**
My Uncle Gordon. Smaller and neater. Ran the Purus office
**Hilda, nee Stock**
His wife. A bastion, corseted and staunch
**Wendy and Janet**
their daughters

**Leonard Eric Innes**
My father, Eric. The youngest son.
A schoolmaster. Tall, muscular, athletic
Taught sport at Handsworth Grammar School for Boys
and later at St Helena Secondary Modern in Colchester
Served in the RAF during WW2

**PURUS BAKERIES of Handsworth**
Founded on a shoestring in 1900 by Charles Innes and his brother Fred. It eventually had 17 delivery rounds, shops and a cafe. It survived into the 1950s, retaining some of its horse-drawn vans almost to the end.

# *. . . Concerning Family*

## *LONDON*

**Alec Raymond Soal**
My great-uncle Ray. Greengrocer of Lewisham.
Younger brother of my late grandfather Leslie.
**Louie, nee Jones**
His wife. Warm and hard-working
**Dorothy and Audrey**
their daughters

**Winifred Gladys Soal**
My great-aunt Win. Older sister of Ray.
A typical auntie. Everyone should have one.

**Violet Annie Soal, nee Jones**
My grandmother, Vi. Of loving heart and sensible mind
Widow of Rev. Leslie Soal, Minister of New Malden
Baptist Church

**Violet Winifred Innes, nee Soal**
Her daughter. My mother. Schoolteacher and actress
Wife of Eric Innes

**Lily Wadey, nee Jones**
My Great-aunt Lily. Younger sister of Violet
As loving and sensible as her sister.
**Francis Reginald Wadey**
Her husband. A big-hearted man. Survivor of Dunkirk
**Reg and Joyce**
their children

**The Scattered Double-Great Soals**
Surviving siblings of my great-grandfather Edward
including Mary, Sarah, Ernie, Edie and Ruth
All with interesting and far-flung careers

# *A thought.*

*'I wish it need not have happened in my time.' said Frodo.*

*'So do I,' said Gandalf, 'and so do all who live to see such times. But that is not for them to decide. All we have to decide is what to do with the time that is given us.'*

*JRR Tolkien:*
*The Lord of the Rings*

*Part One*

# *Birmingham*

# *One*

Mummy knew everything. God made her 'bright and beautiful' as it said in the song. She was 'wise and wonderful' too, and taught me to read and write, and sing and dance, and how little seeds turned into carrots and lettuces. The world was full of magic.

Reading meant I was clever, and Mummy was clever to teach me. Her cleverness, she said, was God's reward for hard work. Mine was a kind of madness, which I caught from my father. The Innes family all had clever-madness, she said, and one day I would have fits like my cousin Pat. Not soon, but later, when Daddy chased the Germans away and came home for good.

I adored my mother but I was not to touch her in case I spoiled her clothes. I didn't mind. She was fragile like the china on the mantelpiece. I knew to be careful.

If it wasn't her clothes it was her cat, a lean black tom called Peter who perched on her shoulder or draped himself over it twitching the tip of his tail.

'Not too close, darling. Pussy doesn't like it.'

I stared him out, edging closer. I heard a new word, 'unnatural'. Apparently it applied to me.

Mummy dripped ink onto paper and squashed it to make a pattern. She asked what it looked like, but everything I saw just proved I had the madness. I tried hard to see beautiful things, butterflies and dancers and clouds across the moon, but even they were wrong.

I didn't want to have fits like Pat. She was ten. Sometimes she fell over and wet her knickers and couldn't play with me for hours afterwards. She had pills that took her cleverness away. I didn't want that either.

'Mad people see things that aren't there,' Mummy said, 'and they do things they don't remember. They hit people, and hurt them without knowing.'

I was frightened.

'I won't hurt anybody!' I said, 'I won't! I won't!'

'You won't remember, darling,' she said, 'Don't worry. Mummy will tell you what you've done.'

Some said the war was ending. There were pictures in the paper; thin people with big eyes. No one would tell me why. I would be three soon. I could read quite well, but the words were too long and the writing too small. My mother took the paper away.

### *Innes of Birmingham*

Handsworth Wood lies on the edge of Birmingham, where the houses thin and give way to park and golf course. The wood has been gone for centuries, but in April 1945 there were still farms around the new builds. Cows munched and snuffled behind our back fence, and green corn sprang in sunny fields, away from the blitzed streets of town.

My father's family lived across the Friary Road, in the older busier streets. My two uncles had regular houses, but activity centred on Grannie and Grandad's rambling Edwardian townhouse in the Selborne Road, where Grandad's study was the unofficial HQ of the family firm, Purus Bakeries Ltd. We assembled there for afternoon tea, or sometimes Sunday lunch.

Purus was the first word I learned to read. It was everywhere. Horse-drawn vans moved gently about the streets adorned with the firm's logo of dancing pastry-cooks. It was in newspapers, on billboards, and spread across busses and trams all over Birmingham.

I loved Grannie's house, the grandfather clock, the ornaments, the patterns on the Persian carpets. Sometimes Grannie took my hand and we fed Biddy, the parrot who lived by the French doors. We scratched the top of its head or made it speak. I felt privileged to be there so it wasn't hard to be good, like being in church, where you felt something wonderful might happen any minute. It didn't, but the waiting was the best bit anyway.

There were special rules for being with Grannie Innes. Children didn't speak to her unless she spoke first. She had been a schoolteacher and didn't smile and laugh like other people. She was old, too, nearly seventy. She wore navy dresses with pin-tucked fronts, and lace at the neck. She sat very straight in her chair, and everyone else followed suit. She watched me with an eagle eye. So did Mummy.

I sat quiet while the grown-ups talked, concentrating on my posture, and remembering what they said. Not that I understood it. If Grandad was at home things were noisier. He joked and laughed with his sons, had eager discussions about the wide world, and played with children. Mummy disapproved of him. She said so. Often.

My mother disapproved of her own family too. They were Londoners. They were common, she said, and did not speak properly, except for Grandad Soal, who was in Heaven now because he was too good for this world. We visited them sometimes to show how things should be done.

### *Soal of New Malden*

My London grandparents, Vi and Leslie Soal, had moved west when they married in 1914. They settled in Minehead, Somerset, in a house overlooking the bay. My mother, Win, was born there, half way through the Great War, while Leslie was fighting on The Somme.

Leslie Soal was raised a Particular Baptist, and returned from France deeply troubled. In a crisis of faith he trained for the Baptist ministry, gaining his first congregation in Overseal, Derbyshire. Win was five. She had her primary schooling in Overseal before the family moved on to Yorkshire; first to Bradford and then to Chequer Road Baptist Church in Doncaster, but she missed Minehead desperately and sought the coast all her life.

Win attended High School in Doncaster and later, as she started teacher training, Eric Innes arrived from Birmingham with a letter of introduction and a post as Gym Master at the Central Boys' School. He and Win were engaged within a year.

What Win really wanted to do was act, and while at college in Leeds she met the film star Robert Donat and developed a lifelong fantasy around him, of which he may not have been aware. He was not her first obsession, nor her last, but they remained in touch until his death in 1958.

Robert fostered Win's ambition, fully supported by Eric, although only they knew that. Her father would not have approved.

In 1937 Eric won the post of sports master at his old school in Birmingham. Win, now qualified, took digs in Handsworth and a post at a local primary school, and Leslie Soal was offered the living at New Malden in Surrey, not far from where he and Vi had grown up. After 23 years they came full circle, back to their wider families, brothers and sisters, nephews and nieces. They couldn't have been happier.

New Malden Baptist Church was a pretty building with a red tiled roof, an arched East window and a tiny bell-tower with miniature spire and it was there, in August 1939, that Win and Eric were married.

Bride and groom set off for Devon but, within days, Win changed her mind about marriage and returned to New Malden. Her parents were furious, the Inneses puzzled, and Eric bewildered and hurt. Win settled back home as if her wedding had never been. She talked constantly about Robert Donat, until her horrified father ordered her to return to her husband.

There followed a series of bizarre events of which I knew nothing for fifty years, which was possibly just as well. Win went missing for several days but returned suddenly to Birmingham where she and Eric helped evacuate schoolchildren for the next two weeks.

Then in short order, war was declared and Eric called up into the RAF. A few months later Win tried to leave the country as Nanny/help to the Donats, but failed to get a visa. Instead, with Eric away, she went south again and spent much of the next year with her parents in New Malden. It was while she was there, one sunny teatime in August 1940, that two waves of German bombers came out of a blue sky and let loose on the town. They destroyed houses and shops, fractured the gas main and machine-gunned passengers at the station. More than fifty people died.

The Baptist church was a ruin, windows blown out, a hole in the roof, and tiles fluffed up like feathers. It was dangerous, out of bounds, and beyond repair, though Win crawled in secretly and took precious photographs. By the end of the month the true London blitz began.

### *War and work*

The loss of the church meant the end of Sunday services, but the rest of Baptist life in New Malden went on. There were youth groups, women's groups, bible studies, Sunday Schools and groups offering practical help. They met in school halls, church halls, scout huts, and private houses, their use offered willingly and irrespective of denomination.

Leslie Soal preached alternate Sundays at another chapel, sharing with its minister to afford them both rest. As air-raid chaplains they crawled into wrecked and tottering buildings tending the trapped and injured as efforts were made to free them. Nobody got much sleep.

Through Robert Donat, Win found work as a film extra. As the blitz raged she, played a Salvation Army girl in “Major Barbara”, filming at the Albert Hall, and worked for the Ministry of Information. Her obsession with Robert continued. She was convinced that, although Robert didn't know it himself, he loved her, a tragic devotion she could only return with friendship.

The Soals were worried. Robert was only the latest in a list of such fantasies, but she had married Eric. They thought it was different. They realised they were wrong.

When Eric had leave, it was Win's duty to be with him, and his duty to be with his family in Birmingham. They made her welcome, but Birmingham was not a happy place to be. The New Malden raid had been a taster, a swift reprisal for Germany's losses in the Battle of Britain days before.

The aim now was to destroy our seat of government in London, the industrial heartlands to the north, and the morale of the people, forcing surrender. It didn’t work, but Birmingham, and nearby towns were in the thick of it, with Coventry virtually destroyed.

Win may have been disturbed in her thinking, but was never lacking in courage. She put on a pretty good show, helping out, baby-sitting the Innes grandchildren and hairdressing for her sisters-in-law.

As bakers my uncles, Harry and Gordon Innes, were exempt from call-up, but did duty as Wardens. Bread was not rationed, but the hours were long, good flour was scarce and fancy confectioneries few. Then a parachute land mine drifted casually down and went off fifty yards from the bakery. Win would have taken photographs but was not allowed near.

My Uncle Gordon wrote:

*"I went up to investigate. [...] the mass of twisted girders and fallen beams, the piles of broken glass which littered everything, the cascades of water from the emergency storage tanks'[...] pouring their contents over flour and machinery; [...] Fortunately, the stables were on the other side of the bakery. The horses there were calmly standing among the litter of blown-in boards; not one of them received a scratch. And we had voluntarily gone over to day baking. Otherwise, there would have been a full staff at work; as it was, the place was empty."*

Eric returned to his base in Northern Ireland, and Win went south and back to Public Information, playing factory girls, housewives, cyclists, waitresses, hairdressers, and anything else they threw at her. They were tiny non-speaking roles but it was all camera experience.

The families were worried. Nobody knew where Win was half the time. It was unseemly. Doctors were consulted, who said that since marriage had not settled Win down, the answer had to be motherhood. A well-meaning campaign of persuasion began. In 1940 women had the vote, they had more than one ground for divorce, but that was about as far as choice went.

### *Domestic soldiers*

Whatever pressures to motherhood Win had from the family it was nothing to the propaganda delivered to women in general. The government had designated women as 'domestic soldiers' and viewed maternity as part of that role. They increased antenatal care, hospital deliveries, advice pamphlets, clinics, etc. all eagerly received, but accompanied by pressure to have babies as a matter of future national security!

It was asking a lot. Through 1941 call-up continued. Bombing continued. Hitler had mopped up most of Europe and North Africa and was heading for Russia. Japan was moving in on Asia. Menfolk were away, friends and family dead or injured, homes and belongings trashed. Who wanted to bring children into a world gone mad? Many did, of course, but not enough for 'the war effort' seemingly. Maternity was becoming a public duty rather than a private choice.

Rations tightened too. Food, clothes and fuel required coupons, and most other things were in short supply. So the government made pregnant women a 'priority class' and awarded them extras. On production of a medical certificate there was orange juice, cod liver oil, vitamin A and D tablets, an extra pint of milk a day, an extra half ration of meat, and an extra egg.

This Welfare Foods Scheme was planned through summer of 1941, along with a bill allowing the conscription of women. Perhaps that's what swung it for Win. She needed control, and she'd have more as a mother than as a conscript. After a brief break she would employ a nanny and resume her film career. That was the plan.

Whatever her reasons, Eric had leave in October and by the time he returned to his base the deed was done and I was on my way. Just in time too. The National Service Act (No 2) was passed in December just as the pregnancy was confirmed. The families were delighted, and Win claimed her new green priority ration book from which my bones still benefit.

In the event married women were exempt from conscription, but Win was now on a one-way ticket to motherhood. At least she had her extra rations and the relatives were off her back. In fact she was flavour-of-the-month in some quarters and enjoying the attention. She gave her due date as 28th May, kept up her film work until she began to show, but eventually made her way back to Birmingham to book her bed and prepare for her baby.

Leslie Soal, meanwhile, and other men his age had fought in a 'war to end all wars'. Now it was happening again. He struggled with his faith. Privately he held to Calvin's dogma of total depravity, where all but God's elect were hell-bound, but he was trained as a General Baptist and preached as such. He tried to give hope to his flock and wrote special sermons for children, which I have in his own hand.

In air-raid shelters Leslie Soal said prayers, sang music-hall songs, and played pat-a-cake with toddlers. But the black corners of his memory troubled him. With long hours, snatched meals, and constant grief around him he developed a stomach ulcer.

Win continued her obsession with Robert Donat. Her parents found this disturbing and with Leslie awaiting surgery they took her on holiday to Somerset. She had filled out somewhat but it was hard to believe she was eight months pregnant, which, of course, she was not. They visited old haunts, went bird watching on Exmoor, and tried to reconcile her to her future. They hoped she would settle once her child was born. She smiled sweetly, told them she loved them, and went on talking about Robert.

Win's claimed dates hinted that Robert might be the father of her child. He was not. I did not put in my scheduled appearance on May 28th, but Leslie Soal was admitted for surgery. Three days later he was dead of a major heart attack.

The Baptist manse at New Malden was, and still is, No 3, Selwyn Road, and there, in the first days of June 1942, it seemed that time stood still. The war was poised to go this way or that and Leslie Soal was dead. By day the house was busy with supportive friends, but in the quiet of night

Vi realised she not only had no husband, but no income and worse, no home. The manse was tied to the ministry. What now?

Win arrived from Birmingham, exhausted, grieving and heavily pregnant; and angry. It was all Vi's fault. Destitution was what she deserved. Relatives tried to calm Win down but she was inconsolable. Vi was shocked and hurt but, as she told me years later, she realised suddenly that there were women all around her who had lost husband, home, and income, even children. It jolted her into action.

The church elders organised the funeral while Vi wrote, to the Trustees asking how long she could stay, and to Southern Railways asking for work. SR had nothing for her but the Trustees said she could stay in the manse if she would take care of it for them. She had a small widows pension. She could manage for a while.

With confinement imminent Win cancelled her Birmingham bed and booked one locally. So I was born in the Wellington Nursing Home, Thetford Road, New Malden at 20:00hrs, 10th July 1942, in a thunder storm. Eric got leave in time to register me himself. Father's occupation reads AC2 3579***, with (schoolmaster), in parenthesis as an afterthought.

So I wasn't born a Brummie after all and I confess to sometimes being a little disappointed. I've never had a Southern mindset, though I did try. I didn't get a Brummie mindset either. Like a jelly in a heatwave, my mind has never set at all.

# *Two*

My mother stayed in New Malden for our first six weeks before returning to Birmingham and the flat over Purus Bakeries. Nearby bomb damage had filled the place with dust. Half the street was rubble. It was no place for a baby. The Ashcombe Avenue house, bought for my father on marriage, was new and not quite complete. It was mothballed at the start of war, but being beyond the Friary Road it was safer from bombs. Grandad Innes with willing help, and leftover materials had the new house opened and the basics decorated in time for Christmas, so at six months old I went to live in Handsworth Wood and stayed for the first five years of my life.

*Memory One*

*Held upon my mother's knee, facing outwards. Her skirt is slippery. I am insecure. Before me is a brown square with a black circle in the middle. A thin man in brown tweed bobs up and down behind the brown square, sticking his arm out and waving a small yellow fluffy thing. Suddenly he throws a black cloth over his head and disappears. I lurch forward and almost fall off Mother's knee. Panic.*

*Perhaps just minutes later. I lie in the pram. The hood is up. The rain cover is on. I can raise my head but I can't sit up. Light tapping sounds begin on the cover. Stretching my head up I see dark spots appearing slowly on the navy cover. They start to overlap. Soon all the light parts will be gone. Fascination. A woman puts the storm flap up. Now I see only her, as she pushes the pram. Her hair is dark and shiny and rolled neatly back all round her head. She puts on a scarf. I want her to look at me but she doesn't.*

I was fifty-two before I found the photograph among my mother's papers though she always denied its existence. The date on the back is November 1942. I was four months old.

The picture was for an agency, my mother's sleek fancy hairstyle only for that day. I was part of the deal. My first publicity shot. I'd have been a cert for startled baby roles, but Mother's discomfort is obvious. She was always reluctant to hold me, but I think it's more complicated than that.

This young woman has been running back to her parents in London ever since she married three years earlier. She still dreams of being a film star. War has intervened, and is at its height. Her father died five weeks before the baby was born. She is in living in Birmingham: in a flat owned by her in-laws, in a street half obliterated by a bomb.

Train journeys between the cities are through ruins and rubble. Families live in sheds and tents beside the track. There are soldiers everywhere. Her old family unit is gone. The pre-war world is gone. The glamorous future is up in smoke. She is assembling several escape plans, but there is really nowhere to run. Her cousin Joyce says Mother hated touching me, and I think it shows. As for me, wide-eyed and lurching forward, I'm only interested in where the man has gone with the fluffy chicken thingy!

*Memory two*

*I am lying back on my father's arm feeding from a bottle, which is boat shaped and has a rubber valve on the far end that lets in air. Sunlight, distorted by the glass, casts a heart shape on the surface of the milk, which sways and jiggles as I suck. Close to my left eye is my father's jaw. There are tiny spikes coming out of his skin, mostly dark but a few are red and catch the light. To the right my mother stands in a nightie woven in wide pale stripes that change between peach and lavender as she moves. I want to see all these things at once. I turn my head as she moves away and choke on the milk, which runs down, under my ears and round the back of my neck.*

Babies know little of war, being concerned mostly with a full stomach, a clean bum, and somewhere warm to sleep. But the sleeping gets less with the dawn of curiosity. I had seen rain, and sunlight, and whiskers, and glimmering silk. Concepts of 'what?', and 'where?', invaded my mind. I just needed words for them.

### *Fits and freaks*

By early 1943 we were settled in Ashcombe Avenue. My mother was disappointed not to have a nanny, but she slotted herself neatly into Innes life, babysitting, hairdressing, and famously adapting and tailoring pre-war clothes into glamorous creations. She became not only popular, but indispensable.

My Uncle Gordon Innes and his wife Hilda had two daughters, Wendy and Janet, who were five and two when I was born. They were bright, healthy, and rather quiet. Uncle Harry's daughter Pat was more demanding. She was eight, and something of a prodigy. She could read at three, wrote poetry, and showed signs of genius.

Then, around the time of my first birthday, Cousin Pat had a fit, a sudden, shocking grand mal seizure, and pretty Pat became the family pariah. The shame, said Grannie, and the damage to business! Pat was consigned to the Midland Nerve Hospital and came home mostly at weekends.

Cousin Pat's epilepsy hung over Grannie Innes like a portent of doom. There were, and still are, many myths and fears around this condition and in the 1940s the stigma was even greater than it is today. Not only was the reputation of Purus Bakeries at stake, but the family's social standing and position at church. Grannie felt deeply ashamed. Epilepsy was a sign of God's displeasure. Grandad's eccentricity suggested his bloodline might carry some sinful taint. Pat became a guilty secret.

My Mother declared that epilepsy was hereditary, and must be in the Innes blood. Not only must Eric carry it, but so must I. She made a plan. Undeclared epilepsy was ground for divorce. When the war was over she would set herself free.

### *Purus Bakeries*

The Purus records are in Birmingham City Archives. Through both world-wars Grandad produced a magazine for staff serving overseas. He employed their wives and daughters to help them make ends meet. He wrote biographical notes on them in the margins of ledgers; their wounds, their deaths. In times of peace he took the entire work-force to the theatre; to musicals, Shakespeare, ballet, and orchestral concerts. The world was a magical place and he wanted to share it. At heart he was a big kid, as was my father.

From a business point of view the Inneses made a great team, and Purus Bakeries throve throughout the war despite bombs and shortages of staff and materials.

Uncle Harry was the practical one and kept the machinery running. Uncle Gordon, by his own admission, was useless as a baker but good with numbers. He kept the books, and paid the bills and wages. Grandad handled personnel and publicity and Grannie dealt with all other legal and business matters. Her word was law and second only to the word of God.

The word of God was that disseminated by the Canon Street Memorial Baptist Church, with which Purus Bakeries had an almost symbiotic relationship. Grandad was an elder, his sons ran the Boys' Brigade and taught Sunday school.

Good Welsh Baptist wives were found for Harry and Gordon and Grannie kept them close, lest they be influenced by Grandad, who she saw as a dangerous eccentric, along with my father. They 'discussed' matters of religion and philosophy. They quoted in Latin and Greek. Grannie blamed education. There was nothing to 'discuss'. It was all there in the Good Book.

My Grannie Innes was brought up as a Particular Baptist by an uncle and his Welsh wife. Her education was a no frills, no nonsense affair, driven by the protestant work ethic. She became a teacher herself and had no time for fripperies in learning. As the youngest son, Eric would not inherit the business. His Grammar School education was meant to be the booby prize and lead him to the ministry. It backfired.

## *Words*

When my mother was born in 1916 Granny Soal bought a Baby Book to record her milestones. There are pages for weights, teeth, first steps etc. Later, she and my mother added notes on me.

As soon as I had teeth I talked; in whole sentences, mimicking, repeating. On the First Words page Granny has written "Elizabeth: at 18 months she could repeat 18 nursery rhymes by heart unaided."

I remember! I remember how happy it made me to learn and repeat what people said, though it didn't always please grown-ups, which puzzled me.

Words! I had words! They told you what things were and what was happening. They told you 'where', and sometimes 'how' though someone might have to show you as well. Words were exciting. Some of them rhymed, but best of all were the words that had tunes and if you could copy that it was called 'singing'. Mummy did it a lot.

In the spring of 1944 my father came home on leave. The back door was open and sun slanting across the kitchen quarry tiles when a man in a blue overcoat appeared, grinning. There is a special kind of thump that a kitbag makes when it hits the floor. This one was white with a purple stripe round it and black letters. I knew him right away. Daddy!!!

## *Tantrum One.*

Tantrum was another new word. It felt nice to say, but it wasn't a nice *thing*. It was a bad kind of being cross and involved shouting and stamping and banging things with your fist. I had them because I was little, which was all right, and Daddy had them too which wasn't. Mummy never had them. She just talked sharply and slammed doors.

Daddy and I had a tantrum together about an egg. I'd eaten my breakfast and was playing by the fire, when my mother brought him a plate with *two* fried eggs. I wanted one. I wailed and stamped. Bang! Daddy's fist came down on the table. The cruet jumped. He shouted. I screamed. My mother returned from the kitchen with her own plate and egg. Now Daddy was shouting at her instead.

‘Whose egg is this? Whose?’ Bang! The fist hit the table.

The ration was one egg per person per week, if you could get them, and the extra egg was mine, not hers as he had thought. He scooped me off the floor and sat me on his knee at the table where he wiped my face with his blue hanky, and let me dunk fried-bread in his yolks.

Daddies, I found, also let you play in mud. We made a lawn, and Mummy didn’t mind. I helped pick up rocks and broken bricks and put them in the barrow. Later, the grass arrived rolled up in slices and Mummy laid them out on the ground and let me jump on the edges to make them stick.

### *London*

Daddy went back to RAF Limavady and we went south to visit Other-Granny. I must live with her now, Mummy said, because she had to go away and be a film star.

I didn’t like the Underground. There were lifts and escalators and tunnels and crowds, and people living on the station platforms. Granny carried me on her arm. The sooty smell made me feel sick so I put my nose under her lapel. The tops of the tube-train windows were open and there was a dreadful noise. Cables on the tunnel walls rushed by like wiggly wormy things. Some of them had got in and were hanging off the ceiling with people catching hold of them.

We visited a place called Seaside and saw a house where nobody lived, and all the furniture was covered in sheets. This was called Auntie Lizzie’s House, but Auntie Lizzie was in Heaven now like Grandad Soal, so we didn’t see her.

We did see the sea though, but couldn’t go near it because of something called ‘mines’. It smelled nicer than London and Other-Granny said she did like to be beside the seaside, and sang a song about it as we walked along the ‘prom-prom-prom’ where the brass band played ’tiddley-om-pom-pom’ in the days before the war.

It was cold and windy and the trees had no leaves, but beyond the barbed wire I could see beautiful grey-green water, rolling over itself. I could hear it swishing. Far away on the other side of the water, Granny said, there was another Seaside called France.

I heard a new long word in New Malden. Precocious. It had something to do with me, and might be a Bad Thing. I was baffled. Remembering rhymes and songs was 'clever' remembering what people wore, or the Latin names of plants was 'precocious', and remembering where we'd been, who we'd met and what was said was 'wicked', but I didn't know why. I was twenty months old and nobody knew what I'd say next.

### *Tantrum Two*

I was still small enough to use the high chair, although it was a tight fit. We were having lunch when the row broke out. I couldn't live with Other-Granny after all. She was still in the manse but needed to get a job. My mother was furious. Going out to work was 'common'. Granny had no shame. She might have known. etc. etc.

I was drinking from an orange plastic beaker, loving the way light shone in through the sides, when the row distracted me and I bit instead of sucking. A tiny crescent of plastic broke off, dropping behind my teeth. Mummy pulled it out with her finger, slapped me hard across the face and slammed out of the back door. I was too shocked to cry and anyway I couldn't seem to breathe.

Granny held my face against her cool frock. She held a spoonful of carrots aloft saying 'Down the little red lane.' and I let her feed me because it was comforting. Over her shoulder I could see Mummy walking away down the garden, pulling washing off the line mechanically, dropping it on the ground. Suddenly she was back. Picking up the chair with me in it, she dumped it in the front room. It was tantrum time.

I screamed and kicked. I bashed my fists on the tray until they hurt and rocked the chair from side to side. Nobody came. Then I found I could rock the chair over quite a long way and it would pause before dropping back. The room was quiet. The blinds were down; slivers of sunlight down their sides. Perhaps I could make the chair stay slanted. Then Mummy stomped past the open doorway wearing her hat and coat. I lost concentration and the chair fell.

I can't have been hurt because I next remember going home. The train was crowded with soldiers, crouched in the corridor with their bags, lifting me from man to man as Mummy clambered past. I used my newest word 'condensation' It was on the windows. They said I was clever. They had prickly uniforms that smelled funny, not like Daddy's flying jacket, which smelled lovely and was furry inside. They passed me round and hugged me. One of them said he was practising and I went to sleep on him.

### *Digging and dancing*

Back in Birmingham as summer began my mother was 'Digging for Victory'. I wasn't sure whether Victory was a person who wanted Mummy to dig on their behalf, or something buried in the ground, which she had to find and I hoped *wasn't* a person. What did come out of the ground were plants, some of them edible. On sunny days we took a bowl of water onto the lawn and washed tiny carrots and ate them straight from the ground and spring onions, which were hot.

Best of all were the pink and white radishes called French Breakfast. I knew from Other-Granny that French people lived at another 'seaside' over the water. That must be what they ate in the morning. I had toast and Marmite myself, and a glass of milk because we were British. Mummy said French people made nice clothes and scent, but ate frogs and snails, and were not to be trusted. Apparently they said 'wee-wee' when they meant 'yes'. Obviously a rum lot.

There were peas in the garden too. We ate them sweet and straight from the pod. Exploring on my own one day, I helped myself. Mummy made me sweep up the empty pods. She was really cross, so I was tidier next time and left the popped pods on the plants. She was still cross but I didn't know why. You can't be in trouble for eating up your peas can you?

She was even less pleased when I helped myself to the radishes. Unwashed. Why bother? A quick rub on the dungarees would do. I just wanted to make her sow more so that I could watch them grow like the mustard and cress on the kitchen window sill; little brown and black dots that split and made leaves for sandwiches.

Indoors we danced to the "Music and Movement" programme on the wireless. I learned the hand and foot positions for ballet from a book with pictures of steps. Mummy made a special board with blocks and pegs to make my feet go out sideways. There were holes and outlines for the five positions and when she had fixed my feet to it and stood me up I had to pull my legs straight holding the arm of her chair. It hurt my knees and ankles, but she was angry if I didn't try, so I pretended it was OK.

On the day I managed my first 'pas-de-chat' she was so pleased I got a hug. Soon, when I was two, she said, I could go to dancing class and learn how to be famous, whatever that was. There were pictures of a famous little girl on the nursery wall. Her name was Shirley Temple.

# Three

Cannon Street Baptist Church overlooked Charles Innes's eccentricities. He owned Purus Bakeries after all. He controlled the money. He hired and fired. He donated generously. Throughout the war he continued his business with horse-drawn vans, supplied manure for allotments and avoided petrol rationing. He was funny and warm, eccentric and sometimes maddeningly irresponsible. He had a white moustache, wore his hair just a little too long, and ties with big soft knots.

Grandad took great joy in life but was sometimes described as 'childlike' meaning he didn't subscribe to Grannie's buttoned-up Calvinist restraint. This she had instilled in her two older sons, though not my father. Purus employees saw Grandad as a 'character' but at home he was an embarrassment. He was a shrewd businessman, but his greatest failing was unthinking spontaneity.

### *Light in the darkness*

It was around my second birthday that Grandad Innes showed me glow-worms. One evening he took his MG out to turn the engine over, and check on his retired horses in a field on the edge of town. There he spotted the glow-worms and, determined that I should see them, he let himself into our house, wrapped me in a blanket and made off into the night.

It was exciting; my first adventure. The night was warm. I snuggled up in the passenger seat. The top of the car was down. There were stars. In that wartime blackout the only other light was a bicycle lamp in the footwell, shining up past my bare toes and onto Grandad's white hair blowing forward onto his face.

The glow-worms were under a hedge in a paddock. Grandad put his trilby down on the dewy grass and lowered my feet into it. Then he turned off the lamp. There, among the leaf-litter, were tiny specks of light, moving a little, flaring occasionally. I stood there in my nightie, on Grandad's old hat and everything was silent but for horses breathing somewhere in the dark.

I don't remember the journey back, but woke next morning on the chaise-longue in their drawing-room, still wrapped in the blanket from my bed. Grandad sat by my feet. Around us was mayhem.

My father was home on leave. Grandad had phoned early to say I was safe, shocking my parents, unaware until then that their baby had been stolen away. The tall Innes brothers milled about the room, Daddy and Uncle Harry in their tweed jackets, and Uncle Gordon neat in a suit. Between them my tiny mother zipped about like an angry wasp shouting up into their faces. They shouted back.

A vast mirrored chiffonier doubled the size of the room and the number of people in it. It seemed very crowded. Suddenly the shouting stopped. The green curtain on the back of the door slid aside on its rod and Grannie Innes entered. There was utter silence, and though my memory doesn't extend beyond that moment, it showed me that women had power, and I grew up wondering why the world pretended otherwise.

Grandad had behaved irresponsibly, and was in trouble, but I think he turned his attention to me after the tragedy of cousin Pat's epilepsy. Like her I was advanced for my age and, in a world at war, he wanted to show me all the joyful things that were still to be found. To me he was the source of my Scottish ancestry; the man who sang "Nickety-nackety noo-noo-noo." and "Keep Right on to the End of the Road." and let me eat the backbones from his sardines.

### *Good mousekeeping*

Mummy said she was going away and I was to live with the Inneses, and while Daddy was still on leave she came home one day in a uniform and said she had joined the WRNS. There was a big row and later two more WRNS came and took the uniform away, which was a shame. I thought she looked very smart, with a shoulder-bag and all.

So Mummy didn't go away after all. My father went back to RAF Limavady and I was enrolled for dance lessons, and

Sunday school where we looked at pictures of Jesus and sang songs. My favourite was "Aubrietias great and small" because we had some in our rockery. Meanwhile Mummy took to training mice.

The mice lived in a glass-sided box on the kitchen table where the cat sat staring at them and jittering his teeth. The many-coloured mice stood on their hind legs, paws against the glass, and jeered. Sometimes Mummy let me hold one. I had to hold my finger out to be sniffed so that it wasn't frightened.

One day I met a mouse that lived under the compost heap. It had a long thin nose and bright eyes. I held out my pinkie. Snap! He clamped his jaws onto my finger-end. It hurt, but I kept very still waiting for him to let go. His top teeth were on my nail, his nose tipped back, and whiskers quivering. The teeth were beautiful and tiny as pins. I watched him until he let go leaving a tiny drop of blood on my fingertip. I didn't tell Mummy in case she caught him and put him in a cage.

The indoor mice, meanwhile, were taken onto the lawn and trained to run through lengths of pipe. They had harnesses made from old leather gloves and attached to a reel of thin twine fixed to a knitting needle stuck in the grass. The cleverest ones learned to thread the twine through longer and longer pipes. They were put in a separate cage and a man came to collect them. It was great fun but I've never quite worked out what she was up to.

### *A new magic*

My father took me to Sunday school the first time, while he was still on leave. As we sang the teacher pointed to marks on a banner, a bit like the ones on Daddy's kitbag. I asked. He said they were words.

WORDS!! Oh my! I knew you could hear them, and say them, and think them silently to yourself. Now he was telling me you could *see* them? Oh joy! The excitement was immense, like a crazed dervish whirling around my brain. I still get goosebumps remembering how it felt. I needed to know more. Fast.

There was a mark for every sound, big and small versions, and different ways of making them. The kitbag ones were stencils. They said “INNES”. Daddy showed me “Innes” on envelopes where grown-ups joined the marks up together with flourishes and curlicues. Oh give me more!

I saw words everywhere now, on walls, on trams, on shops ... even clothes. One day I saw our name high on a billboard, with a picture of a bear. ‘Innes!’ I shrieked, only to be told it said “Guinness”. Ah! So the extra curly bit on the front said “Guh”. I made a mental note.

I became such a pest that my mother taught me to read. One day, she reckoned, books would keep me quiet. It worked up to a point. Eventually. Meanwhile, I learned the alphabet and she hung words on the furniture. There were cards that said “door” and “chair” and luggage labels on small things like “handle” and “broom”. My favourite was “cupboard” because you didn't say all the letters, and you had to be clever to know the ones to leave out.

Writing was more challenging but I persevered, drawing rows of m and n and b and g, loops that were open, loops that were shut, tails that went up and tails that went down. Paper was in short supply. I wrote in mud, and in sand, and on steamy windows. Grandad gave me a blackboard. It was a new magic and I couldn't get enough.

I had yet to learn how dangerous words could be.

### ***Practice to be perfect.***

When we weren't dancing or writing we practised things you had to do when you were out. It was called rehearsing. Not ordinary things like staying close to Mummy, or not making a noise at Grannie's. These were special things where I had to spot a signal from Mummy. If she squatted down with her arms out I was to shout ‘Mummy!’ and run to her. She would scoop me up in her arms and I could kiss her cheek. (She couldn't kiss back because of the lipstick.) If she tidied my collar or smoothed my hair it was a sign to look up and say, ‘I love you, Mummy.’ and remember to smile.

I enjoyed rehearsing. It meant I could touch her; and I got to run the whole length of the hall and be hugged. It was important, she said, to show everyone how much I loved her, and what a good Mummy she was. It worked too, and people always looked pleased when we did it in company. She even smiled herself. At other times it wasn't allowed.

My mother didn't smile at home, and if I smiled at her she looked away. I spent a lot of time in the pram. The comfy pram of my baby days was long gone, replaced by an ugly second-hand tub of a thing into which I was strapped and left round the back of the house. Mrs. Yates from next door talked to me through the fence.

'You're a bit big for a pram, aren't you?' she said one day. I agreed. 'Did Mummy forget you?'

I wondered if I could persuade her to let me out but Mummy came out, raised the hood and tightened my harness. I couldn't sit up so I just watched the sky and the birds that came and sat on the pram handle. There were butterflies, and a bee who came and went to a hole between the bricks. I was learning to count, so I tested how far I could get between his visits but I didn't know enough numbers.

I started talking to these little companions until Mummy took to putting a sheet over the whole pram. After that I just had to talk to myself. To be on the safe side I learned to whisper. I told myself what I thought the birds and butterflies were up to outside, and realised I could see them in my head if I wanted to. In fact, if I closed my eyes, I could see anything I wanted. So that was all right. I had no idea what a prison that pram would become or for how many years.

### *Winter war-work*

A time came when it got dark before bedtime. The big trees outside the back fence went to sleep and their leaves fell off. The mice retreated to the nest-holes at the back of their box, and even the cat stopped waiting for them.

It was too cold to train mice outdoors so after tea my mother sewed faces on dolls; just the faces. The dolls were soft, and looked like modern teletubbies. They came in a box that someone left in the garage at night. I could hear the latches. The dolls were ready-stuffed with fluffy white kapok and Mummy tied a scarf round her nose to stop her sneezing.

The painted faces were stiff moulded cloth, and stood in a stack on the arm of her chair. In another box were little shiny cylinders. She tucked one into each doll's head before she sewed on the face. She said they were a special surprise and I mustn't tell anyone in case the Germans heard me.

I knew what Germans looked like. They walked with their legs stuck out in front. There were pictures in the paper and Mr. Giles drew them in the cartoons. They were very dangerous. Some of them were so small you couldn't see them, which is why you had to wash your hands so often. They hid in lavatories and got in your food. Other German's were big and had guns. If you were killed you went away to God and couldn't come back again and if I was naughty God would let the Germans kill Daddy and it would be my fault.

So I tried very hard to be good but it wasn't easy. There were more and more things to remember. Not nice things you could pull out of your mind for fun, but things that mattered every minute like how you sat or stood or placed your hands. I tried to sit properly with ankles neatly crossed but always had to be rearranged, especially my fingers. I learned lots of new words and letters and practiced my dancing. By Christmas I could curtsey, and do my pliés, and even a "ronde-de-jambe-en-terre".

Everyone said how clever I was, how grown-up I was. I took life very seriously. I was two and a half years old, going on twenty. My father told me years later that when he next came home his happy pixie had turned into a grim little prodigy who had forgotten how to play, and he knew there was no going back.

### *Things that go bump.*

We went south for Christmas, initially to Other-Granny in New Malden. Granny had made a cage under the table so we didn't have to sit in the cupboard. On our earlier visit she had been at work one night and we hid under the stairs while things went bump outside.

I lay in a basket with my legs over the edge while my mother sat on the shelf with a night-light in a saucer. She sang "I Know my Love by his Way of Walking,". I remember the door shaking but not the bumps. Just the sound of the singing and the night-light flickering on Mummy in her blue satin housecoat with the round quilted collar; and her hair tied up in pink chiffon. She looked so beautiful I couldn't be afraid.

Now why was a parson's widow working night shifts, at that time? Granny Soal's WW2 ID card is among the family papers. It tells much. It is blue, rather than green, and is a replacement. The first stamp is dated 4th March 1944. She will certainly have had an earlier one issued c1939. The card is in three parts rather than two, and includes a photograph, hair and eye colour and height. What is going on?

It is the card of someone working officially under the War Department, in this case a railway employee. The photograph was signed by Southern Railways' Chief Assistant, (Signals and Telegraph), based at Waterloo Station, where Granny worked. From March 1944, at night after the last passenger train had run, Southern Railways were secretly moving men and munitions into position along the south coast in preparation for D-Day. Signals and Telegraph eh? So that's what Granny was up to in the dead of night, and presumably why she never talked about it.

The new cage was, in fact, a Morrison Shelter with a plate-steel top and mesh sides. It held a double mattress and Granny slept top-to-tail with us and let me tickle her toes with mine. There were no bombs though. Bombing had stopped. Even doodlebugs had stopped. Now it was V2 rockets, none of which fell on New Malden. For Christmas itself we went to Lewisham, near the London Docks, where it was another matter entirely.

That Christmas morning I worked out the truth about Santa Claus. Mind you, I'd had my suspicions. I'd had a brief interview with him in a big shop, called Bentall's at Kingston. The room was full of lights and we queued with a lot of other people. He asked me what I wanted to be and Mummy told me to dance and show him my pas-de-chat. She told him I was going to be a star like Shirley Temple. I was too young to be embarrassed, but I did fancy a red coat with white trimmings.

I asked him about the apparent multiplicity of Santas. I had spotted several others in passing. Apparently, pre-

Christmas Santas were substitutes because the real one was so busy. My question caused some consternation, but I was just trying to work out what grown-ups really believed, and what they pretended to believe for fun.

### *The curious case of Santa's boots:*

I already knew that the Germans and the doodlebugs were real because of the broken houses I could see from my pushchair. That was why we had to sleep in Uncle Ray's cellar in the Ladywell Road. There were a lot of us, and we were a family. Granny explained.

Grandad Soal had been Uncle Ray's brother. Auntie Win was his sister. Auntie Louie was his wife and their children Dorothy and Audrey were Mummy's cousins. (Another new concept.) After that it got difficult. Granny's sister, Auntie Lily was with us, and her children, Reg and Joyce who were also cousins to Mummy but not to Dorothy and Audrey. I gave up. Too much information.

There were ten of us in all. Every available bed had been marshaled and crammed together in the cellar, where they rocked and creaked and occasionally collapsed as people crawled across them to reach their own. My mother and I had a strange wood and canvas concertina contraption, which had been mended (frequently) with a great deal of string. My mother got little sleep but I slept like a baby, because I still was a baby, or so they said. I thought I was pretty big really, but grown-ups wouldn't be told.

Uncle Ray was a greengrocer and despite rationing and shortages, had plenty of in-season homegrown produce; carrots and sprouts, onions in strings, and leeks as thick as my arm. There were chestnuts, sold in brown paper bags, which he twirled with a flourish. Earthy potatoes rumbled into a big brass pan to be weighed. The smell was wonderful.

The Lewisham people were different from the Birmingham ones. They talked faster and loudly. They sang silly songs and laughed a lot; and they hugged and cuddled and sat me on their knees while Mummy snatched me off and made me stand in case my dress creased.

Granny became impatient with cousin Reg who told me that the dangerous things on my hands weren't Germans, but germs and hand washing did nothing for the "war effort".

Reg couldn't be a soldier because he had a bad chest, but he wore a big overcoat and a tin hat with letters on and went out at night looking for bombs. He said Santa might not come, and was told off.

'Listen,' he protested, 'The sky's full of planes and rockets. He can't use his lights. If he tries it he's a hero or an idiot!'

'He's a hero!' said Granny curtly.

In 1944, with most of the men away, and everything in short supply, Christmas was a matter of ingenuity rather than indulgence. On Christmas morning, cups of tea were handed out from the cellar steps and when everyone was settled Reg announced Santa Claus. It was Santa all right. Coat, beard and sack of gifts all present and correct. He stood on the steps above us as everyone unwrapped their homemade gloves, socks, pincushions, lavender-bags, and precious jars of Pond's Cold Cream.

My present was last of all. A double bed made from an orange-box, sanded and stained brown. A coverlet crocheted by Granny and two small dolls, one white, one black, complete with nighties and bed-socks.

I stood on the bed as Santa handed it down. My eyes were level with his feet. He was wearing ... (*Sssh! I'll whisper*) ... Uncle Ray's boots. Of course I didn't let on. It would spoil it for the grown-ups.

# Four

I enjoyed Other-Granny and the Lewisham relatives, even though Mummy said they were common and a bad example. I enjoyed their noise and fuss, their laughter and the way they did things together. Anyone could make a pot of tea, even men.

Different people wiped my face or did up my buttons or put me to bed. There were ten of us in the cellar at night. The ladies took off their dresses. Other-Granny even took off her *teeth*, which made her lips wobble when she snored.

I was only frightened once. There was a big bang and dust came out of the ceiling. Mummy pushed me under a blanket so I wouldn't breathe it. The light went out. Cousin Reg came back in the morning with his overcoat dirty and said there'd been a rocket but not too close. He looked upset and went to sit outdoors on his own.

There was a row because Mummy took me on the bus to see if there was fire. I remember a street blocked off with oil drums and planks and the road stretching away beyond, littered with bricks and slates. A lady hung out of a window. Someone went up a ladder to help her, but she fell. The man at the barrier shouted at us to go away.

Records show that a V2 rocket fell in Kitto Road on 6th January 1945. It was some way away but the shock wave would have reached us in the cellar.

### *All around the houses*

Christmas was long over when we went home to Birmingham. My father's New Year leave had been cancelled. Something came up. The RAF was busy and it was almost spring when Daddy next came home. His uniform was very smart.

I wanted to impress him. I smoothed my skirt carefully when I sat, made sure my back was straight, crossed my ankles neatly, and checked the position of my fingers. Daddy kept looking at me strangely and I thought I wasn't doing it right. Eventually I burst into tears. Mummy took me off and clipped me into the pram in the front room.

Undecorated and unused since the house was built, the front parlour housed the pram, the ironing board, some tea-chests and my mother's fret-saw. This apparatus was worked by a pedal, and with it my mother turned bits of wood into wondrous things. She glued pictures onto plywood and made me jigsaws that would fit on the little tray across the pram. There was no jigsaw that day. I wept and wailed.

There was shouting. I waited. Suddenly, my father came in, still in uniform, jammed my pixie hood on my head and trundled me out of the front door while my mother squealed at him down the hall. He was grinning. I stopped crying.

Ashcombe Avenue is a close, a neat circle of semis. My father wheeled me, publicly, once round the circle. It just went to show, said Mummy, that the Innes family was mad. No man in his right mind would be seen wheeling a pram, she told him, 'It's the epileptic disposition.'

We went round to Grannie and Grandad Innes later and Mummy had me sing the new song she had taught me.

*"Let him go, let him tarry,*
*Let him sink or let him swim.*
*He doesn't care for me,*
*and I don't care for him."*

They smiled, and I carried on unaware that it was a taunt.

... and where were my toys, my father asked? Where was the board with the coloured pegs and little hammer he had given me? And what did I get for Christmas? All unsuitable, declared my mother, and not educational, and one of the dolls was *black*. Daddy did some shouting.

To be honest I hadn't missed toys. I loved the reading and the dancing, and singing songs, and listening to Gracie Fields or Paul Robeson on the wireless. Otherwise I liked to watch things; my mother's hands as she folded clothes or wrapped parcels; the drip and smell of sealing-wax; little beetles in the lawn; the rolling-pin spinning across pastry. Sitting alone in the pram wasn't nice, but sometimes there was a spider to watch. I liked spiders.

### *Hammer and nails*

My father had other ideas. He was a gym and sports teacher by profession and knew the value of exercise. Dancing was all very well, he told me, but I needed my little hammer to make my arms strong. He took me into the yard and introduced me to a pin-hammer, a box of tacks, and the block we used to chop kindling. That kept me quiet for a bit. Then he gave me the pincers to pull the tacks out again. I had to use both hands. I felt really big and strong.

Next Daddy fetched a box of old keyholes, washers, and escutcheons and we made patterns with them on a railway sleeper using screws. Oh my goodness! You didn't bash screws. You had to make a little hole first.

'This,' said Daddy, 'is a bradawl.'

A delicious new word; I could feel it rolling round my mouth as I spoke.

'If you want her to use her arms,' said Mummy, 'she can do something useful.' She set a bowl of soapy water on a chair and I washed Daddy's socks. I pegged them on my own little line and Daddy took pictures.

'Girls do *not* do woodwork.' Mummy said.

'So what about the fretsaw?'

'*That* is not woodwork. It is handicrafts, and is called a hobby.'

What a complicated world this was!

Peter was hurt. Mummy's black cat had run out of luck. I found him yowling pitifully by the rockery one morning. One of his ears was almost off and there was a big tear inside his back leg, red and pink against the black fur. My father took him to the vet. He came back alone. Peter had been in a fight, he explained, and another cat had hurt his wee-wee parts and they couldn't be mended so he'd gone to heaven where God would stop it hurting.

Mummy was hysterical. Wicked, wicked Daddy had killed her lucky black cat: On purpose: To make her upset. I didn't want to believe that, but I wanted to comfort her, to make her feel better. I just didn't know how.

'Why did it look like meat?' I asked cheerfully.

'Because you could see the muscles.' said Daddy.

I had muscles. I wondered if we ate cats or people. Mummy said, 'No. Just cows and sheep and pigs.'

'and whales and horses.' said Daddy

'Eric! *Please!*'

The conversation ended just as it got interesting.

### *Health and beauty*

In 1926, when my father was eighteen, his parents put him on a banana boat and sent him to teach for two years at a mission school in Kingston, Jamaica. Grannie hoped it would lead him to a life in the church. All it did was broaden his horizons. He discovered a warm and accepting form of religion, with laughter and lots of singing. He was never the same again.

Daddy was detailed to take me to Sunday School as his punishment for having the cat put to sleep, but he didn't take me to Cannon Street. He took me to a hall where almost everyone was black. Whole families said prayers and sang and children danced to the hymns. There were people from Jamaica who knew Daddy and made a fuss of me. It was another small rebellion on his part, a demonstration like wheeling the pram round the close. He knew I would tell Mummy where we'd been.

Daddy had gone again. The trees grew new leaves and we went exploring. There was a door in the back fence that led into a field. In the far corner was a pond. We kept frogspawn in a jar of water. It turned into tadpoles. They grew legs and we put them back to let them be frogs.

I was stung by a nettle, but Mummy said we mustn't cut them down because the butterflies needed them. She had a picture of a Red Admiral and I knew it from my time in the pram. There were all kinds of butterflies. Some had wings with orange ends and some were blue and very small. I didn't like commas though, because their wings were brown and untidy, and I couldn't say 'fritillary' at all.

I missed the cat. I missed his big green eyes and the way his claws slid in and out of his toes. My mother missed him more. She was used to having him on her shoulder all day and took to wearing one of her dead foxes instead. She had a ginger one she wore with her camel coat, but this one was black with silvery bits and could clip its mouth to its tail. I suggested we get a live one but she said they bite.

Instead she fetched a box from the back of the wardrobe and showed me a pair of shoes. They were red. They tied up with ribbons, and had shiny metal bits underneath. She put them on and danced across the kitchen going tickety-tickety-tick on the quarry tiles while the man on the wireless sang, "Keep young and beautiful." (*tickety-tick*) "It's your duty to be beautiful." (*ker-chunk!*)

I could have watched her forever. It was called tap-dancing and I would be three soon and could learn to do it too. Red shoes! RED SHO-O-O-Z! We went to the dance school and watched some big girls doing it all together. I could hardly wait.

### *Going to the zoo*

Suddenly, people were saying the Germans had gone away and the war was almost over. We just had to tidy up something called Japs, but they were too far away to send bombs. Mummy was jubilant. She had a dead bird with long wings we found in the garden and turned it into a bluebird for her hat. I knew about bluebirds. They flew here over the White Cliffs of Dover somewhere further away than London.

Other-Granny came up for my third birthday in July and gave me a special present, a pair of shiny black shoes with metal taps on the toes. I wanted to go to dance class right away but people were on their holidays. Mummy said I'd never be a real dancer because I was mad like the Innes family. Granny said not to be silly. Then we went to Dudley Zoo.

We went on the bus and my mother wore her dead bird hat, very small with a veil. She had painted the bird blue with ink and whiting and put two wax cherries in its beak. Granny said it might have crashed into her head and was bleeding from the mouth. Mummy made a bad face.

The bus was packed. I sat on Granny's knee but Mummy refused all offers of a seat.

'We never sit down on a film set,' she said 'in case we crease our clothes.'

And Granny said, 'You're not on a film set now, Win, so for goodness sake sit down.'

The lady next to us admired the bird. I said, 'It's a swift actually. Daddy found it by the compost heap.'

Mummy turned her back and gripped the overhead rail.

One long wing of the bird pointed straight up and as the bus jogged and rolled, we watched it flick to and fro against the rail above, showering pale blue powder down the back of her neighbour's navy blazer.

There were lions at Dudley and Granny said she knew someone called Albert who'd been eaten by one. Mummy said it was just a story but there were people called lion tamers who could go into the cage. They were very brave.

Bravery was important, I knew. If I could prove I was brave maybe she would stop saying I was mad. I just needed to get myself some lions.

### *Stamp of approval*

Stamping wasn't usually allowed. It was a sign of tantrum and a Bad Thing, but when you had your tap shoes on it was different. I liked that. There would be a concert at the dancing school, and if I learned my first dance properly I could dance for lots of people, not just the family. The dance was Irish.

I knew where Ireland was. RAF Limavady was in Ireland. There was a globe on my father's desk so I knew the world was round and I could find the British Isles quite quickly. Everything to one side of it was called The Continent where people didn't speak English, and the other side was called America, where they did. Beside America was a tiny red island called Jamaica where Daddy had lived long ago. I could find that too.

I pictured myself tapping and spinning and bending and waving my arms like Mummy did, and was disappointed to find that I had to keep my back straight and my arms stiff at my sides. This was because Irish people only danced from the knees down.

I reckoned it must be how you recognise them. So Germans walked with their legs stuck out, the Irish danced from the knees down and there were people called Top Brass that Daddy said were dead from the neck up. I wanted to know if they danced too and he said 'Only to their own tune' and everybody laughed.

The concert was in a church hall with a proper stage and curtains. I would be dancing alone. I practiced walking to the exact middle, not looking at the people, and concentrating on my steps. I had a dress of blackout material and a green apron and cape and I promised not to be scared. Shirley Temple was *never* scared. So anything she could do ...

At three there was no sign of the crippling stagefright that would assail me later in life.

# *Five*

The footpath near Uncle Harry's house was of black and red bricks with bumps like a bar of chocolate. Some of the bumps had a cross on top to stop you slipping. The street always smelled sooty, but once beyond the gate I could smell the earth; because I was nearer the ground, Uncle Harry said.

There were big shiny leaves under his front hedge called bergenias, and frilly ferns, and cushions of tiny leaves with a name I couldn't say. (*Saxifrage*) and all along the sides were black tiles with edges like rope.

It was autumn, Mummy told me, and would soon be winter. The squirrels would go to sleep. The butterflies would roll themselves in leaves and wait for the sunshine. I had to wear my pixie-hat outdoors and people lit their fires. We had a gas-poker for ours.

We had a pushchair too and sometimes Mummy took me round to Auntie Rosa and forgot to collect me. Then Auntie Rosa wheeled me home, and Uncle Harry was cross because his tea was late.

### *1945: Fits and frights*

Sometimes cousin Pat was home from hospital. She had fits. I knew she couldn't help it but it made me sad. Mummy said it would happen to me one day and I would have to live in hospital too. I thought I might not mind as long as there was singing and dancing and Squirrel Nutkin and Peter Rabbit.

Mummy said the mad Inneses gave her bad nerves. I was sorry that God gave her a child like me. I worried about the fits too. I didn't want to wet my knickers, like Pat did. Mummy said you didn't always have fits. There were other signs of epilepsy, other ways to tell if you were mad. You imagined things that didn't happen, and you didn't remember things that did.

She said it was in my blood. I asked her to get it changed for good blood but she said we couldn't because the devil had hold of my soul. I knew better than to argue, but I felt angry. I didn't need Mummy to tell me what I did or saw. I was good at remembering. I would just have to make sure I remembered everything, and knew whether it was real or pretend.

We had tinned apricots for tea that day. I concentrated. They sat in the custard like three bright egg-yolks and when I turned them over there was a hollow underneath. The bowl was cream with orange and yellow flowers on the rim. I fixed it in my mind and later, in bed, I described it to myself so that I couldn't possibly forget.

I asked my Sunday-school teacher what a soul was. She said it was what made you “YOU”; a piece of God's own soul that He put in when you were born and it went back to Him when you died. I said Mummy told me Satan had hold of mine. The teacher said I mustn't say bad things about Mummy.

I'd have to be brave all on my own then. I just needed to get hold of some lions.

### *Good wives*

Uncle Harry had good reason to need his tea on time. Although Uncle Gordon worked office hours, as did Grandad in his elder years, Harry was the Master Baker now, and rose at 4:00am to see the first loaves into the ovens. He went early to bed. Auntie Rosa was happy to minister to his needs as Auntie Hilda was to Gordon's. That was what the world expected of them: selfless dedication to the needs of men. If they had other skills or experience I never knew.

There was obviously something seriously wrong with my mother, so I don't think greater freedom would have fulfilled her, but she was creative and talented in many ways, and a wonderful teacher. Her elders felt it was their duty to keep her in line. It crushed her and even my father's efforts on her behalf were to no avail. He too was under pressure.

There had been a fire at the big bread bakery, so during rebuilding they used the old one, which was smaller and harder work. Mummy took me there. It was hot inside. There were two iron doors in the wall and men in grubby singlets were fishing out trays of hot bread with long wooden shovels.

There was a scrumptious smell and a soft crackling sound as the crusts cooled.

Mummy asked why the men had no shirts on.

'It isn't a fashion parade, love.' they said.

And Mummy said, 'I'm Mrs. Eric to you!'

We went to the main bakery then, where they made the cakes and pies, and Mummy left me by the engine. It popped and rattled and made a great din as the belts whizzed off through holes in the wall driving the machines. A word on the engine read 'Tangye' but I didn't know how to say it. I was there for a long time. A man in an overall came. He sent for Auntie Rosa. She wheeled me home where Mummy was washing her hair. Auntie Rosa never shouted when she was cross, but I knew she was.

### *Doctor's visit*

Mummy wouldn't go to the doctor for her nerves, so Grannie sent him to the house. His name was Campbell. I hid. I'd met him before when he vaccinated me and made a mark on my arm that was *never* going away! Mummy didn't want to see him either and used her high voice to make him leave. He said a baby would make her feel better.

We went to Grannie's for afternoon tea. The aunts were there. Grandad was chased away for saying 'secret midnight hags!' Mummy said she wasn't making more mad Innes children. Grannie said Wendy and Janet didn't have fits and Mummy said it was only a matter of time.

Auntie Hilda said, 'If you've got two perhaps you'll remember where you left them.'

Granny gave her a funny look. Auntie Rosa was quiet.

I was by the parrot cage, trying to memorise the colours of feathers when suddenly Mummy was pointing at me.

'There you are! What did I tell you? Petit mal! Petit mal!'

'Calm down, Win,' said Grannie, 'the child was just daydreaming, weren't you Elizabeth?"

I said yes I was. I watched as Biddy shelled a peanut with beak and tongue.

'You may choose a little boy yourself, Win,' said Grannie, and to me, 'Wouldn't you like a little brother, Elizabeth?'

Mummy said, 'Over my dead body.'

I panicked. I could do without a brother. I didn't want Mummy to die. I screamed and pleaded and Grannie sent us home.

### *Let there be light.*

Blackout curtains came down in every street. A man with a pole rode round on a bicycle lighting the lamps at dusk. Everyone would be coming home.

'Not everyone.' said Grandad Innes. But we were all to look our best so that men knew what they'd been fighting for. Mummy had her hair permed.

At the hairdresser's I sat beneath a washbasin with a colouring book for hours. In the tiny cubicle Mummy was wired up to an overhead collection of china dingle-dangles on cords. The smell was horrible. And just when I thought it was over they washed her hair again and put dozens of pins in it, and long curved clips with teeth. She sat under a hood with cotton pads over her ears and couldn't hear me for the noise. I promised myself never to have a perm. There were better things to do with half a day.

Anything you could burn was used to eke out the coal ration so there were no bonfires on November 5th, but there *were* fireworks. Daddy got leave and couldn't make the Catherine Wheels go round, but he fired rockets from a milk-bottle and helped me hold a sparkler and draw light-pictures in the air. Mr and Mrs Yates came from next door and we ate ginger cake, and baked potato with real butter. Lights blazed all round the close, until a warden turned up and said just because the blackout was over didn't mean we could waste juice. Daddy grumbled, but otherwise everyone seemed happy for a change.

I slept in the nursery now, and had my cot under the oriole window, with the side down now that I was big. From there I could climb onto the sill and see all round the circle of houses. One foggy morning the milk cart emerged from the mist with the horse dressed up black and shiny with white furry feet. He was festooned with brasses and had poppies in his mane and tail. The coal horse and Grandad's bread-van were the same when they came later.

Daddy had gone again but everyone else was at Grannie and Grandad's later. We heard Big Ben and had to be quiet for two whole minutes. Grandad cried and was shooed out of the French doors. I ran after him to lend him my hanky.

They didn't let me talk to Grandad usually, since the incident with the glow-worms, but I found him in the garage with his red MG. There was another car there, covered in old eiderdowns. He said it was time to clean it up and take it for a spin. Maybe when I got my new brother.

Oh no! Not that again. I told him it could only be over Mummy's dead body and what would I do without a Mummy. He said that was a 'figure of speech' and not true. What was a 'figure of speech'? Was it a pretend then, I asked, or a lie? He told me to ask Daddy. He would come home to stay soon, now the King didn't need him in Ireland.

### *Where Jesus lives.*

Life was busy. There were ballet and tap lessons and practicing at home. There was singing at a candle without making the flame flicker, and now there were sums that Mummy made up, adding tens and units. I knelt on the floor with a chair for a desk and devoured them by the dozen.

There was usually something going on, but when there wasn't I was alone in the pram in the front room. The harness was enlarged with string and when it was tightened I couldn't sit up to read. I had finished my Beacon reader anyway. The sky had fallen on Chicken-Licken, and the Gingerbread Boy was long gone, but Daddy had read me poems by A A Milne so I just lay and practiced them to myself.

*'I am Sir Brian, as bold as a lion ...'*
Mummy asked if I would ever be quiet.
*'The King asked the Queen*
*and the Queen asked the dairymaid...'*

It seemed not.

* * *

Then suddenly he was there: Daniel, a little boy, on a visit. He was two and a half and very thin. His poor pale chest stuck out in a ridge and he couldn't talk at all. He was simple Mummy said, but his eyes didn't look simple to me. They were huge and blue, deep blue, like the cornflowers in the garden. He came from a children's home and couldn't live with us until he was fatter. Mummy put him in the pram and we walked and walked until it was nearly teatime.

The day darkened. It would soon be Christmas again. There were packages in the pram, and a roll of fancy paper on top of a beaver skin the Indians gave Auntie Lizzie in Canada long ago. It was stiff as a board, with sharp edges and a bit bald in places, but Mummy thought it a glamorous cover.

We had just turned a corner when Daniel got his finger stuck in the beaver's eyehole and as Mummy disentangled him I noticed across the road, a great red disc, low in the sky beyond a tall fence.

'What's that?' I asked.

'It's the sun,' said Mummy, 'He's going to bed.'

I asked who made the sun. She said, 'God did.'

PING! Of course! God's only sun, I thought. That must be where Jesus lives. I looked round for the name of the road but couldn't see it. The house was over to the left, a grand house of red bricks with its name high up on the wall in big letters and not difficult to read.

It said ASTON VILLA.

### *A shadow on the moon.*

My father soon set me straight about The Son and the sun, and laughed about Aston Villa. He told me about football, and said he would be back at the Grammar School soon and I could come and watch. The sun, however, was a globe like the world but it was on fire so that we could see and keep warm, and yes, he reckoned God must have made it because he couldn't think of anyone else clever enough.

We had been reading Winnie-the-Pooh at bedtime but one night Daddy asked if I wanted a Pooh story or a True story. I opted for True. He fetched his globe and a tennis ball and with the bedside lamp for the Sun he showed me how it shines its light on the moon, and the moon goes round the world, and once in a very long time the world gets in the way and makes the moon look funny. It was called an eclipse.

'And,' he said, 'it's happening tonight. If you go to sleep right now we will wake you up to see it.'

I was far too excited to sleep, but eventually my parents stood me on their bedroom window-sill and I watched the shadow creep over the moon until it turned the colour of meat and then slowly reappeared, round and yellow and glorious. They left me then, alone in their bed with the curtains open as the moon rose higher and higher and I wriggled closer and closer to the edge so that I could still see it. I woke in my own bed next day under a spell. I knew something special. The sky had changed forever.

### *A Soal perplexed*

Other-Granny was coming for Christmas. I sat in the pram colouring paper doilies while my mother painted the front room around me, stenciling terra cotta patterns on a base of peach distemper, or stamping them with shapes cut in halved potatoes.

I looked forward to Other-Granny's visit. I was pondering a mystery. Inside my body was a 'ME' made up of bits that 'took after' other people, and a soul which, according to my Sunday school teacher, was part of God's own soul that He gave to us. God's soul must be pretty big, but where was it? Up in the sky? Like heaven?

(*Thinks!*) A sole! Ah! That was it! a huge footprint, out beyond the stars. I peered through the nursery curtains at night but couldn't make it out. Granny was a special sort of Soal. She would know.

As Mummy did her Christmas baking, I played with pastry scraps. I broke off little 'souls' and rolled them into balls. I lined them up and then squeezed them back into one lump. The scraps grew grey and grubby. Mummy gave me more scraps, clean and white. I squashed them together and started breaking off bits again: but what was this? The new 'souls' were marbled grubby and clean, old and new: another mystery.

On Christmas morning there was a green velvet dress with frills and rosebuds, a book "Little Grey Rabbit", and another picture book of foot and arm positions for ballet. Mummy declared the Innes presents unsuitable and despite Other-Granny's protests I was not allowed to see them.

Granny said I should have fun as well as learning. Daddy said he was going for a walk.

For lunch there were sprouts with crosses cut in the stalks. I cut them carefully now that I used a knife and fork. I found a silver pig and a threepenny piece in my pudding. There was holly everywhere and Granny told me about Jesus in the stable. I asked if there had been a war on then and Daddy said, 'Sort-of'. Mummy told him not to use slang. Then we listened to the King.

Soon, it seemed, we were eating again; tiny sandwiches, fruit jelly, tarts and cakes. There were second helpings and nobody mentioned rations. I sat up to the table on several cushions feeling very grown up.

The tea-plates were square, cream with silver tracery and flowers in one corner. There were cake-forks with one wider prong, and a special knife in the butter. A three-tier cake-stand, palest green with a pink lustre overflowed with pastries, more beautiful than any present. All around us the walls glowed with Mummy's designs. Everyone was happy. It was time to ask my question.

'Granny,' I said, visualising the footprint in the sky and God chipping bits off the edges, 'God puts a bit of his soul into new babies doesn't he?'

'Yes dear.' Granny beamed.

'and when people die it goes back to Him doesn't it?'

'That's right.' The grown-ups looked pleased.

'So when God breaks off a piece for a new baby he must sometimes use bits he's used before.'

Granny's ringed and freckled hands froze over her plate.

Daddy said, 'The transmigration of souls!'

Mummy said 'Eric!' very sharply.

I filed the new word away for later. Transmigration. People liked you to say long words. Someone suggested I might want to go and wash my hands.

I went upstairs quietly and sat on my bed. Had I said something wrong? I mustn't cry. It would spoil Christmas. Daddy came up. 'Have I been naughty?'

'No,' he said. He was laughing, 'but you mustn't frighten Granny like that.'

'Why is she frightened? Mustn't I ask her about God any more?'

'You have very grown-up thoughts sometimes, Elizabeth, and it can make people uncomfortable. Let Granny tell you the stories, but you'd better ask *me* the questions.'

Downstairs, Granny Soal was smiling again and later she tucked me into bed. I laid my face on her cool silky lap, which rustled and smelled of violets, and she read to me about Little Grey Rabbit and Squirrel and Hare keeping house somewhere in the country. I was content. When the King didn't need Daddy in the RAF any more, he'd come home and tell me everything I wanted to know.

# *Six*

After Christmas my father came home more often and for longer bringing strange garments and bits of kit; his beat-up leather jacket with the furry collar, and a pair of vast boots with sheepskin linings that unzipped all down one side.

Grannie and Grandad were proud of him in his uniform. The uncles were not. They said fighting was a mug's game, and called Daddy a chump.

Grannie Innes said, 'That's enough!' and they were quiet.

Although my father was their little brother, he was in fact thirty-seven years old. Harry and Gordon were forty-four and forty-one, but when Grannie gave an order, they obeyed. I thought this might be a Good Thing, though I couldn't have told you why.

### *1946: Knight manoeuvres*

My father was worried by what he later called his 'grim little prodigy', but there were no suitable toys for my level and even drawing turned into writing. What I loved most was words. They are still my mental Lego bricks. You can build things with them, slot them together in all directions, rearrange them, make them happy, or sad, or funny. In desperation he introduced me to chess.

I loved the board with its neat squares, and elegant pieces. I loved the ways they moved, especially the knights, but the aim of the game distressed me. As Daddy explained what I had to do I looked at him in disbelief.

'What's up, chicken?'

One of us had to lose. I didn't want to lose; but I didn't want Daddy to lose either, especially if it was me that won. I told him.

'Cos if you lose you have to be killed,' I said, 'like in the war.'

'It's just a game.' he said.

I asked him if the war was a game and he said, 'Oh Elizabeth.' in a tone I came to know well.

I'm not a psychologist but perhaps three-year-old girls need Daddies to be invincible. He taught me Clock Patience instead where it was just me and the cards; where winning was a surprise and losing meant trying again until it turned out right. But I kept the knights in mind and when I couldn't sleep I pictured the board and tried to work out how many blocks of six squares you could make altogether. There were six one way, and seven the other, twice, but I didn't know enough numbers to count them all, so I fell asleep trying.

### *Speak to me*

I was signed up for classes in acrobatics, so along with the ballet, and tap dancing, and reading, and sums, my days were very full.

Daniel came to stay more often and was definitely plumper. Daddy said he would be well enough to be adopted in the summer. While I did my lessons, it was he who was strapped into the pram now, in the unused front room. Sometimes I was with him. Mummy removed a panel from the floor of the pram and we sat, tied tightly, facing each other across the centre tray, with our legs dangling into its belly.

I tried teaching Daniel to talk. I looked into his huge blue eyes. 'Watch my mouth,' I said, 'Hel-lo.'

'Woo.' he replied.

I tried again, and with 'please' and 'thank you' which I thought might be useful to him. He managed 'psh' and 'koo' but only when I asked him to.

'You're wasting your time, Elizabeth,' said Mummy, 'He's simple. It's called retarded.'

I asked if that was like me being mad. She said it wasn't and left the room.

Alone in the pram, I wanted Daniel to say my name.

'E-liz-a-beth.' I said.

'isspss,' he tried.

'Say luh.' I stuck out my tongue, 'Like this, luh luh luh.'

Daniel banged his hand on the tray and let out a wail.

'Shhh!' I said, 'Shhh!' I knew what that was. It was a tantrum, which was OK because he was little, but if you had one you had to have a nap.

We couldn't lie down so I leaned on the tray with my head on my arms and he did the same, his hair fine and soft against my cheek. I thought he was beautiful and he was going to be my brother. But I did wish he could talk to me.

### *A Whale of a time.*

Other-Granny was fun. She could find at least one laugh a day and had bright brown eyes and a wide grin. Oddly, my mother forbade levity in Granny's presence, because she and Grandad Soal had been close chums with God who didn't like that sort of thing, or so Mummy said. Granny told people it was one of 'Win's funny ideas' and hilarity broke out mostly when my mother was absent.

Before she went home after Christmas Granny took us to the cinema. It was my first time. Some people were swallowed by a whale. I could see them inside. They lit a fire and the whale thrashed about. The screen was huge. The whale was huge. I screamed and screamed and was taken outside. Mummy said I'd spoiled everything. Granny said it was all right and the people would escape. Daddy was irritable.

I stamped my feet up and down on the street. They weren't listening! I didn't care about the old man, or the cat, or the odd looking boy. It was the fire!

My father snatched me up, and I draped across his shoulder sobbing 'Poor whale! Poor whale!' He stopped being cross right away and Mummy said I was weird.

My father explained later that whales couldn't swallow people because they had a sieve in their mouth that only let little things through, and that Pinocchio was just a story and not true.

Like a lie? No, a lie was a trick for a bad reason. Stories were things you imagine in your head and when you tell someone, or write it down they can imagine it too, like Pooh Bear, and Little Grey Rabbit.

So Pooh and Rabbit weren't real? They couldn't wear clothes and live in a house and cook dinner? Daddy said they could be anything you wanted them to be as long as you knew they were pretend.

'Is that why we're the mad Innes family?' I asked, 'Because we imagine things?'

He said, 'No, imaginary things are invisible and can only be seen in your head. Mad people actually see things that aren't there.'

And what was this about the Innes family? I told him. Daddy did some shouting. I went to my safe place behind the armchair.

Mummy used her high voice. 'Look at you!' she said to him, 'Just goes to show. Can't control your temper.'

My father left the room, slamming the door. I resolved to do the same when I was big enough to reach the handle.

My mother didn't have a temper. She had what we now call hissy fits. She tossed her head about and flashed her eyes while her voice went from high and squeaky to low and menacing.

Sometimes Other-Granny said, 'Thank you, Miss Bernhardt. We'll let you know.'

### *Bride and prejudice.*

Another reason for Other-Granny's visit was to make me a dress. Mummy's cousin Reg Wadey was getting married in London and I was to be a bridesmaid. Mummy said the bride was a common 'clippie', a bus conductress, and why ever were Frank and Lily letting him marry her. Granny suggested I didn't repeat what Mummy said as it could hurt someone's feelings, and that Reg loved Margaret very much.

Since the people Mummy thought common were always the most fun I was looking forward to the trip, and the train. On the station platform I braced myself not to jump when engines went 'schoompf'. I was big now. I must be brave. So I didn't hide my eyes as the train came in, and I saw for the first time the wonderful wheels, taller than me, joined by long shiny bars that see-sawed as they slowed and passed my face. I wondered why.

We stayed at Soal's Greengrocery again but not in the cellar since there were no more bombs. Everyone was happy and Mummy didn't stop people cuddling me. They sang songs as they worked. "There was I waiting at the church..."

and everyone joined in. "Why am I always the bridesmaid..." Uncle Frank taught me a special song to sing for Daddy later.

Uncle Frank was Reg's father and had funny turns because he'd been at Dunkirk. He shook and trembled and I was hustled from the room as Auntie Lily lit a cigarette and put it in his mouth. It happened one morning when we were alone. He couldn't keep still. His face was grey. Sweat dripped off his chin. I found a cigarette. Bits came off on my tongue. I tried the lighter and could just get my hand round it but the little wheel hurt my thumb. I tried and tried. I looked at Uncle Frank to say sorry, and realised that in spite of everything, his eyes were laughing.

I'd never seen a bride before. Her red roses covered half her body. Her dress swirled about her like water. I carried my posy carefully and didn't trip over my frock. One of the other bridesmaids shut her finger in the car door. Otherwise all went well and nobody got angry with me.

There were servicemen on the train home, but smart and clean, not like the tired unshaven ones I'd seen before. They held doors for people, and carried cases. Americans. They had different uniforms and called my mother Ma'am. But outside Snow Hill station were the old soldiers, sitting on the ground, drawing with chalks, winding up tin toys to sell, playing accordions, wearing their medals on threadbare jackets. I asked why, but no one would explain.

### *Just so.*

I had to sing my new song. On Uncle Frank's instructions it was a secret, so even Mummy didn't know it. My parents sat proudly as I began:

*'It's a great big shame, but if she belonged to me*
*I'd let her know who's who...'*

Mummy jumped up and ran from the room but my father laughed and laughed until I'd finished. He said. 'I think it's very funny, but Mummy doesn't, so perhaps you'd better not sing it again.'

That was all right. There were lots more songs to learn.

Daddy showed me pictures of real whales, and how they had sieves instead of teeth and then he read me “How the Whale Got Its Throat.” This story told me that in America braces were called suspenders, which was embarrassing because here, suspenders were under ladies' skirts and you didn't talk about them.

The story was by Rudyard Kipling, and there were lots more about other animals, and the pretend things that happened to them. Imaginary animals! You could make them up. LIONS! I could have lions!

The nursery was over the garage. One wall was normal height but the ceiling sloped down on the other side almost to the floor. There was a low false wall across it with a sliding door. Behind it all manner of trunks and boxes were stowed. Ideal. I lay on my bed and covered my eyes. Slowly I made myself two pet lions, and installed them in the nursery cupboard.

### *Tongue tied.*

I was famous for my lions and kept them for almost a year. They were extremely fierce and hard to handle, and responded only to me. My bravery was legendary. Each evening I fed them the crumbs from my tea-plate, accompanied by growling and cries of ‘Back! Back! Down!’

Spring came. Daniel moved in with us at last. My father was demobbed and came home. Grandad Innes stripped the old eiderdowns from his Hudson Terraplane and took us for a day in the country. The car smelled of warm leather like Daddy's flying-jacket, and we had sardine sandwiches and orange juice, and cake from Grandad's bakery.

My mother found a chrysalis and kept it in a jar on the windowsill, where it became a Red Admiral. I wanted to see it fly but Mummy dropped smelly cotton wool into the jar. The butterfly died and she pinned it to a tray with lots of others in a special cabinet. They were going to die anyway she said.

Daniel still didn't speak, and then one day my mother put his dinner-plate in front of him.

‘Hot!’ she said, ‘Don't touch!’

Daniel raised his hand in defiance and plonked it flat on the plate. The heat hit him. His mouth opened wide. He screamed.

Mummy said, 'Look Elizabeth! Look in his mouth! He's tongue-tied!' and sure enough Daniel's tongue was fixed down behind his teeth with the end folded in an odd way.

Some doctors say tongue-tie doesn't affect speech, but I know what I saw, and I'm sure he could not have spoken however hard he tried. He had been in the children's home for two and a half years but they were so overwhelmed with war orphans that there was no time to notice. Doctor Campbell had Daniel's tongue snipped along with his tonsils and he soon learned to talk, but with a stammer that has never left him.

# *Seven*

We were a family now. The King sent my father home for good. I had a brother. Even better, I was his sister. I would look after him. My mother and I sometimes disagreed about this, but I lavished my wisdom upon him unstintingly, and tidied his hair whenever I got my hands on a comb.

Bathing was interesting. Daniel had some extra bits, which you mustn't kick under the water. Apparently this was how you told boys from girls but the bits were delicate. I was glad I didn't have any.

There were so many things I wanted to know. True to his word, Daddy read me Kipling, about the Elephant's Child who lived near the 'grey-green greasy Limpopo River' and had a 'satiable curtiosity' like me, and asked a lot of questions. Granny Innes thought they should not be answered and we should read our Bibles more.

### *How high is the sky?*

In fact the blame at this time lay not with my father, but Irving Berlin. A song on the wireless told me what to ask like *"How deep is the ocean? How high is the sky?"* I knew the moon went round the globe, and the earth's shadow made the eclipse, but why didn't the moon fall down?

Because, said Daddy, it was going too fast to fall, but not fast enough to run away into space.

Space? What was that? He told me about the planets, and how we all went round the sun, and didn't fall because of 'velocity', which was a clever word for how fast we went. There were pictures of Jupiter and Saturn. Saturn! So beautiful! And the stars were other suns far far away.

*"How long is the journey, from here to a star?"* sang the man on the wireless. Daddy said it was so far that you couldn't write it down. There'd be enough noughts to go right round the world. I thought maybe not if you wrote them *very* small. He said not even then.

So how big was space, I wondered, as I lay in my bed, and what was at the end of it? There'd have to be a wall or something, but how thick was the wall, and what was on the other side? I racked my brains and realised there must be stars and stars that never ended, and God must be out there somewhere taking care of it all.

### *The littlest things*

I learned "How Deep is the Ocean?" and sang it a lot.

*"... And if I ever lost you, how much would I cry?"*

I had lost Mummy in Woolworths once and was terrified, so I understood, but Daddy said it was a love song about how grown-ups fall in love and become Mummies and Daddies.

Grannie Innes was cross with him and said you couldn't go falling in love with people willy-nilly and your family needed to choose you someone who could afford a house. If I was very good she'd choose me somebody when I was big enough. Nice kind Grannie, but right now I was interested in the infinity of the sky.

As well as infinite bigness, there was infinite smallness, Daddy said, and like the bigness there were clever people trying to see it. They'd found atoms, which had a middle with bits that went round like planets, and the number of bits told you what it was. There were diagrams called hydrogen, and helium, which were special sorts of air with only one or two bits.

Atoms joined up to make other things and I pestered to know them all until Daddy said, 'I can't tell you any more. Wait till you go to school.'

It was something more to think about in the night. Just supposing, I thought, just supposing the world and the planets were part of an atom in a button on a giant's coat. I suggested this to Grannie Innes who said I would be a "blue stocking". Uncle Gordon said I would grow up a "collar and tie job" and Daddy said I could be whatever I wanted.

Granny said 'Not in *this* day and age' and he said it wouldn't be *this* one.

Whatever were they on about? Oh well, if atoms were all right with Daddy they must be OK. Meanwhile he sang to us sometimes instead of a story; of a man who was stolen by the Queen of Fairies and rescued by his girlfriend; and a girl who wouldn't marry her family's choice and ran off with Jock of Hazeldene? I learned them. I'd have to wait for atoms, but meanwhile there were songs.

### ***Let the children play.***

Towards the end of summer the monstrous pram was loaded onto a train and Mummy took us to Clacton-on-sea where we stayed at 'Skeena', Auntie Lizzie's house. Other-Granny came down from London. Great-great-auntie Lizzie had died and Granny was going to live there instead, and look after Auntie Mary next door, another of my great-grandfather's sisters.

Granny promised us fun in the sand now that some of the mines had been cleared, but when we got to the beach we had to stay in the pram and not get dirty. Granny protested. Mummy was dismissive.

We watched her dig in the sand and make shapes with a bucket. Then she placed us carefully for a photograph; Daniel in his shiny patent shoes and me in a dress that mustn't touch the sand. Granny humphed and tutted and said that wasn't what we came for. Mummy was cross and flounced off.

We spent many hours at Skeena after that, parked out of sight in the pram, from which Granny freed us frequently and let us play in the street, or sweep the yard with real grown-up brooms. Finally my mother relented and although we weren't allowed on the sand, we rode carousels and donkeys and ate our first ice cream. The sun shone, and if it rained at all I didn't notice.

I tried to tell Other-Granny about 'escape velocity' but she just said, 'My Goodness! Whatever next!'

Other-Granny didn't know about atoms. She knew about food, and could make wonderful things out of almost nothing, like tripe and onions, or cauliflower cheese, and the best Welsh Rarebit in the world.

Back in Birmingham I was soon to start school. My father would take up his old post as sports master at Handsworth

Grammar School. He took us there one day and showed us the class-rooms; the desk he sat at when he was twelve, his initials carved under the lid. Everything smelled of chalk and disinfectant.

We walked through the changing rooms, which smelled of leather and something like Daddy's socks, and on into the gym. My heart leapt. There were wall-bars and ropes and beams and mats. Daddy took off his jacket and swung over a pommel horse. 'Bit rusty,' he said, 'Need to put in some practice.' I wanted to learn.

'Girls don't do that,' said Mummy, 'Girls dance.'

Of course. Never mind. I loved dancing.

### *First class.*

I don't know how long I lasted at Cherry Orchard School; a day perhaps. I only remember the first few hours. I knew what to do. I was to call the teacher 'Miss', raise my hand if I wanted to speak, and if I was naughty I would have to sit in the corridor. That seemed simple enough.

It is one of my most detailed memories. The teacher was smartly dressed. Her name was Miss Baldwin. She wore a grey skirt with sharply pressed box pleats stitched down at the top. Her blouse was pale peach and had a scalloped collar with a flower in each corner. Her dark hair was coiled over her ears like earmuffs and she had a bandage on one hand. I concentrated really hard. At last I would learn about atoms.

Miss Baldwin held a small blackboard against her side and drew a spiral, which we were to copy. Ahah! I thought. It's like one of Daddy's trick questions. I know what she really wants. I drew a circle with a dot in the middle. Miss Baldwin walked among us. I put two dots on the circle.

Miss Baldwin said, 'Oh Elizabeth you are funny. What is that?'

I said, 'Helium, Miss.' and started to write an H.

Miss Baldwin dropped to her haunches and looked into my face. She seemed anxious, or maybe cross.

'Elizabeth, can you read?'

I said I could, and she led me into the corridor where she sat me on a chair and told me to find a book from the shelf. She left me there. I was in the corridor! What had I done?

I must have got it wrong. I only knew helium and hydrogen. Maybe it was the other one. I wanted to explain and say sorry. I found a book and tried not to cry.

Cherry Orchard was a very new school. There was no canteen yet so children had to go home for lunch. I didn't go back that afternoon, but we went next morning and Mummy said it was their duty to feed me, and she wasn't traipsing back and forth all day. She had better things to do, like teaching me herself. So we went home and she did that.

There was a head-to-head battle with the authorities but my mother stood her ground. She threw them chapter and verse of the Education Act, employment of married teachers, plus the rights and duties of all and sundry. She tied them in knots. They gave up.

I did eventually go to school, quite a few schools, but only once or twice did a teacher inspire me in the way my parents did in those short years before it all went wrong.

### *Friends and neighbours.*

However good my home education was it could not provide me with company. There was no time to socialise at my dancing classes and although I had Daniel at home, he was still learning to speak. I recognised a little boy at Cherry Orchard School. He lived in our street and his name was Anthony Parsons. He came to our fireworks on November 5th with his mother and I dared to hope. Maybe I could ask to be friends.

The Yates from next door came too, and the man from the other side who had been in the army and caught a disease in Scotland from eating grass. Mummy said he might poison our lawn and we'd all get it. Daddy said to shush.

The Catherine Wheels spun properly this year and we had Jumping Crackers and Roman Candles and I made my first poem about them. Daddy gave me a notebook from the Grammar School next day and I wrote it out carefully.

I wanted to show my poem to Anthony but everyone said maybe I could play with him when the weather got warmer and meanwhile it was time to learn joined-up writing. Life was all about learning. I enjoyed it and didn't fret about not having friends. I didn't know I was supposed to have any.

We went to the museum to do history and I learned where coal came from, and flour to make bread, and I saw pictures of how metal melts when it gets red hot and brave men pour it out like water.

Grandad let me watch his bakery horses being shod and told me that everything has to come from somewhere, and somebody has to get it or grow it to make it into something else.

Other-Granny came for Christmas again and gave me a dolly's mangle with real rubber rollers. I found a screwdriver and took it apart. Under the cover were two wheels with teeth, and one wheel pushed the other one round; in the opposite direction. The bars on railway engines made the wheels go round the *same* way. I asked my father why they were different so he bought a box of Meccano. I never looked back!

### *1947: How cold my toes (tiddly-pom)*

Christmas 1946 gave us our first real toys, and though Daniel was too small for Meccano he happily pushed Dinky Cars round the room with appropriate noises, and enjoyed taking the tyres off. I was detailed to stop him swallowing them. I expect he swallowed many, as there was always a shortage, but Daddy kept a bag of spares in his desk. We were learning to play which made my father happy, and since his demob we were only strapped in the pram when he was out.

When Daniel chalked on the wall, my mother's clever solution was to paint a whole wall of the nursery black, and give us unlimited chalk and dusters. Heaven help us if we drew on any other wall; but why would we when we could stand on a chair and draw giant cats, life-size people and tall trees dripping with flowers?

I had my lessons, but Mummy sometimes played with us now, and taught us tiddly-winks and marbles. Daniel swallowed one. It would kill him, Mummy shrieked, and why wasn't I watching him? I was, but it was down his throat before I could take breath. Daniel survived, confined to using an enamel potty until a loud clank announced the marble's reappearance.

The weather grew cold; the worst winter anyone could remember. Crops froze in the ground, coal froze in the depots, and even the sea froze in places. There were shortages, and long power cuts. I remember candlelight and huddling round a meagre fire in our coats.

My father brought home a stray dog and called it Rex after a dog of his boyhood that died of poison. Mummy wouldn't have it in the house. We wanted to stroke it, but it had to stay in the shed and we could only see it through the window. It was a typical taunt by cruel Daddy, she said; the man who had her cat killed. She mentioned this a lot. I tried to calm her.

'Peter's underneath parts were torn and he had to go to heaven.' I said.

'Trust you to side with your father! Mad! Callous! All of you! It's in the blood!'

It didn't make sense. If I was siding with anyone it was the cat. Time to go and do a jigsaw or something.

The freeze continued. There was snow. A blizzard such as no one remembered swept the country, piling great drifts in towns and cities. I saw nothing but snowflakes beyond the window, swirling, streaking, suddenly reversing in mid-air, allowing no glimpse beyond. There were shadows in its dizzy depths, dark and powerful like a great beast forever trudging, getting nowhere. I tried to make a poem about it but failed.

In the elms behind the house a tawny owl quietly froze to death. The dog picked it up next morning. Mummy wrapped it in newspaper to keep its feathers tidy, packed it in a big military vacuum flask, and we took it to be stuffed.

It was a major expedition. Birmingham was at a standstill and my mother needed to get herself, two small children and an owl into town on foot. We bundled up and Mummy got the sledge from the shed.

Well-bred children from good families wore gaiters, Mummy said. Christopher Robin wore them, she said, as did

James James Morrison Morrison Wetherby-George-DuPree; the boy in the poem, whose mother disappeared. Mummy bought some second hand, knee-length in thick hide, and hard as iron. The edges pinched as she buttoned them up to my knees with a long silver hook.

With Daniel and the owl-container on the sledge we set off into Handsworth and were half way there when my feet went numb and I fell over.

'It's the gaiters!' I wailed, 'They're stopping my blood.'

'Chin up!' said Mummy, 'We need to suffer a bit to set a good example.'

We met Daddy at the Grammar School where he was clearing snow. He took one look at the gaiters, produced a penknife and ran it down behind the buttons. They shot everywhere. He threw the gaiters far into the snowdrifts and rubbed my feet while the feeling came back.

Mummy explained about Christopher Robin, and Daddy muttered a word, which seemed to mean 'nonsense' and said that Christopher Robin wore gumboots anyway. So he does. I've checked the illustrations. We bought some right away.

And the owl? It was stuffed and mounted on a branch. It looked at me with soft wise eyes, and sat by my bed for several years where I could stroke its breast with the back of my hand when I couldn't sleep.

### *Water, Water, everywhere.*

We were shopping the day the thaw set in. Under the drifts the street-drains echoed with drips. They rattled, they rushed, and by afternoon there were streams and puddles everywhere. The sun shone. The world smelled fresh.

I stepped into the house ahead of Mummy. SPLAT! Beyond the hall my father was sweeping water from the kitchen into the yard. We poddled towards him in happy curiosity. He was very quiet. So was Mummy.

We peeped round the sitting-room door. Dotted about the carpet were bowls and buckets, even the watering can, gathering water that fell from the ceiling in silver strings. The most curious thing was that no one blamed anyone else. There was a job to do. They got on with it; Hot drinks and food for a start.

So it wasn't frightening, it was interesting, and when he'd been fed Daddy lifted us onto the loo seat to see into the cistern. It had frozen, crushing and puncturing the copper ballcock. At thaw the ball sank, leaving the valve open and, with the overflow still frozen outside, the water cascaded onto the floor, between the joists, through the ceiling and down the stairs. Gosh! And all because water gets bigger when it freezes: another of life's wonders.

The carpets had hardly dried out when Daniel and I got measles. It was one of several diseases that everyone had sooner or later. Sooner was best. The others were mumps, chicken-pox and whooping-cough. I don't remember the spots, but I do remember the headache, and the boredom of lying in a darkened room to avoid blindness. Daniel was moved into the nursery with me, but was too poorly to communicate.

How had I caught it, Mummy demanded, had I been *kissing* anyone? Daniel would be blind. It would be my fault. I cried for shame but it made the headache worse.

Daddy said it wasn't true, but when we had our eyes checked later Daniel had to wear glasses and I was upset.

I dictated my diary to Daddy in the evenings because I couldn't write fast enough for my thoughts. I used him like a pen, an object, unaware that I was confessing the secrets of my heart.

'It isn't your fault Elizabeth. Daniel is just shortsighted. Lots of people are.'

'Daddy! You were *listening*! You were listening while I was writing.'

'No. I was writing. You were talking. It has to go through my mind to get to my hand."

'Oh! ... You won't tell, will you? "Not a word to Bessie", I quoted the radio catch-phrase.

'Not a word.' he said.

### *A grown-up decision.*

I was worried about my lions, the ones that lived in the nursery cupboard. I'd had them for almost a year. I'd fed them crumbs from my plate every day. I'd let them sleep under my bed while I had measles so that I could feed them from there. But people had lost interest. I had been famous for my lions, and my bravery. I needed a publicity stunt like Grandad Innes, who, I was told, had done one quite recently.

Grandad's latest idea struck him after hours one Thursday, but it needed cash. With no access to the bank he took the made-up wage-packets from his office safe and used them to buy all the carnations and fern from the flower ladies who sat on the steps of the Arcade.

He sat all night in a new (untaxed and unlicensed) motor-van making up buttonholes, and as soon as the big stores opened, starting with John Lewis, he presented one to each shop assistant, "with the compliments of Purus Bakeries". It was a great idea, but the men were paid late, and irate wives besieged the shop. My father thought it a great jape. Grannie did not.

Access to Grandad was difficult since the glow-worm adventure, but I got a minute with him and he suggested my lions could go mad. I could be even braver handling them and everyone would notice again. So the lions developed a serious problem, which I imagined so well that I became terrified of them and wouldn't feed them. I had nightmares. I had gone too far.

My parents suggested it was cruel to let the lions starve. It might be kinder to put them to sleep, but it had to be my decision. I agreed and Daddy offered to shoot them, humanely, with his starting pistol. My mother sat with me on their bed as he loaded up and entered the nursery, holding a kitchen chair before him. 'Back! Back!' He yelled.

There was growling. I put my fingers in my ears. There were two shots and all fell quiet. I burst into tears. Mummy left me to it.

My father came in mopping his brow with a hanky.

'They were only pretend lions.' I sobbed.

'Elizabeth, we have to take responsibility for what we imagine too. They were your creation. If we imagine things too hard they become more real than we want.'

He gave me the hanky.

'Daddy? Does God just imagine us?'

He said 'Oh Elizabeth.' and went downstairs.

That night at bedtime, we said goodbye to the lions. Squeezed into the long cupboard under the eaves, with a lighted candle and two shot-glasses of orange-juice, we perched upon a kitchen chair. My mother's camel coat with the red fox collar lay over a trunk, for all the world like a dead lion.

Daddy raised his glass. 'This is how they do it in Ireland. It's called a wake.'

'Ah, to be sure,' said Daddy in an Irish voice, 'He was a grand lion, always good for a growl. Oi shall miss him ... Say Slainte.'

'Slainte' I said. And the lions were gone.

### *Show business*

We must do things to make Mummy happy, my father said, so that she wouldn't be upset all the time. I didn't think she could be happy while she had us. He said we'd just have to do our best. He took Rex to the dog's home and got Mummy a black and white kitten she called Patchy. That helped.

The sitting room had dried out and been redecorated. Mummy called in a professional photographer intending to send pictures to Nursery World, a magazine that featured posh families, which meant us, she said. Daddy disagreed.

There was a lot of bickering about how we should be posed and everyone but Daniel was in a foul mood. Including the photographer. Making people happy was really hard work, but I cheered up to pose in a Dutch Girl costume and everyone seemed pleased. I doubt the photographs were ever featured.

The costume was for a dance show in May. The measles had put me behind with rehearsals. If I caught up, perhaps that would help the happiness project. I could never dance like Mummy, or look as beautiful, but if she could be happy, perhaps she would be kind, and stop reminding me I was mad.

My teacher worried that I might not make up time. Last year I had done a brief Irish dance in a community hall, but this was a serious show in a theatre, with lots of numbers and a singing solo for me. Most men were demobbed now, or released from prison camps. Their children had grown beyond recognition. It was time to celebrate, and show what we could do.

The musical numbers were linked to the Allied Nations, “Zip-a-di-doo-dah” for America, “The Little Old Mill” for Holland, and “The Old Lamplighter” for us. We were starting with “Spread a Little Happiness” and ending with “Over the Rainbow”, which was my solo. There wasn't time to be nervous but then, I hadn't seen the size of the place.

The dress rehearsal was the first time I saw the theatre. The safety curtain was down, and behind it dozens of people milled about the stage. It wasn't just our group of little tappers. There were big girls in tutus who danced on their toes, and grown-ups who did their own things. Mummy danced like an Indian lady in bare feet, with bells on her ankles, and made lovely shapes with her hands.

Everyone was busy so I counted my steps to the middle of the stage so that I'd know where to stop for my solo. I was just working out how to keep a straight line when somebody raised the safety curtain.

Oh my goodness! There were seats and seats going back forever, and an upstairs part with gold and white patterns round it. There were lights on the floor with coloured covers and a dizzying drop beyond them to where a lady sat at a piano. With her was a man carrying something strange that made sounds like birds. It was a violin.

I had only practiced “Over The Rainbow” singing along to a record but managed quite well with the piano. Then the man with the violin joined in and it was so lovely I forgot my next breath.

‘Don't be nervous,’ someone said, ‘It isn't an exam. People are coming to enjoy themselves and we're here to help them do it.’ That felt better.

There were no Health and Safety people then, so three four-year-olds with lighted candles and flannelette nighties caused no alarm singing “The Old Lamplighter'”. “The Little Old Mill” went down well too, as the little Dutch girls tapped their socks off.

Somebody complimented my mother on the starching of my hat. I said, 'Daddy says I'm a bit young for a Dutch Cap.' and everyone fell about laughing. Except Mummy. I had no idea why.

Standing in the wings before my solo, the stage looked suddenly vast with no one on it, like the football field at Daddy's school.

(*Remember: Just walk to the middle, turn, and nod to the piano lady when you're ready.*)

I walked. I turned. I was in the right spot, between the pink and blue footlights. I looked up. Oh! ... You could only see the people at the front.

I nodded at the piano. I sang. I remembered my big breath for 'That's where you'll find me.' ... and something happened. I could only see the people at the front, but I could *feel* everyone else. They were *happy*. Not like people at home. The violin flew with the 'happy little bluebirds' of the song and I felt we were all floating.

I don't remember the applause. I curtsied and left the stage, still transported. I'd got it right. I'd made people *happy*! I wanted to sing forever. I still do.

# Eight

We weren't seeing much of the other Innes people. They were busy. Things were complicated at Purus Bakeries. Despite surviving the war unrationed, bread was limited. A disastrous harvest, shortage of manpower and stray mines around the coast meant little wheat.

Mummy often took us for lunch at The Purus Cafe, in the Soho Road, where most things now came on thin toast; sardines, beans; dried egg, reconstituted and scrambled. Being family, we dined cheaply on all the things that had gone a bit wonky. My mother took to sitting us at the table, ordering, and disappearing for an hour or two, leaving the staff to look after us. They seemed used to it.

I enjoyed the kitchen where I indulged my taste for burnt fishcakes (strange child!) and was allowed to load the toaster, a monster with two drawers that took ten slices each, and shot out with a PING! when they were done.

### *The lady vanishes*

On July 10th I was five, and a fortnight later Mummy ran away. I didn't know that's what she had done, of course. (for fifty years!) We just found ourselves on a train with Daddy, heading goodness knew where. The pram was in the guard's van with our clothes.

Daddy hadn't a clue how to pack. He dragged things out of drawers, stuffing them into the pram. I tried to show him how Mummy did it, but there was no telling him.

Despite my interference Daddy kept his temper, and now we were on the train with our colouring books, and wherever we were off to it looked promising. Daddy's sports bag was in the luggage rack and he'd brought his tennis-racquet.

We joined my mother at Skeena, Auntie Lizzie's old house in Clacton. I didn't know what was going on with the grown-ups, but I heard the rows and tried to work it out. In the late 1990s I tracked down my mother's cousin Joyce who told me what really happened.

Lizzie Soal was one of my great-grandfather's six sisters. She died in 1941 leaving half the value of Skeena to her nephew, Leslie, my grandfather. But we were at war. No one was buying or selling houses, so Skeena stood empty. When Grandad died only a few months later, it left a headache for both executors. Granny would leave the manse in New Malden and be homeless, despite inheriting half a house, so ways were sought for her to buy the rest.

A woman alone had little security in 1947, and despite Granny's frequent presence that summer, I now know she was still in New Malden on weekdays and working all hours to raise half the value of the house. The executor was Uncle Ernie, Lizzie's younger brother and he moved heaven and earth to make the purchase possible. An added advantage for him was that Granny would look after his sister, Auntie Mary, who lived next door. Meanwhile Skeena stood empty.

My mother let herself into the house and went the following day to the Registration Office requesting a replacement ID Card. She gave Skeena as her address thinking to start over. The office insisted on her previous address, which she gave reluctantly. The new card is stamped July 26th. By the end of the day, the Office had found Skeena registered as unoccupied. The police were called. They sent for my father, along with Auntie Lizzie's executor. Hence our sudden train journey.

Mummy said she hadn't done any breaking and entering. She had simply picked the lock on the back door, (Something she was mysteriously good at.)

'They teach you that, when you work for MI5!' she said.

Everyone rolled their eyes.

My mother would not return to Birmingham, so Daddy rented Skeena from the executors for the summer and started planning a move.

There were difficult adjustments for many couples after the war. Some had seen little of each other for years, or nothing at all. With my parents, however, the problems went far deeper.

Daniel and I were oblivious. Granny came down from London at weekends and took charge of us while our parents tried to sort themselves out.

### *Widow at work*

When Grandad Soal died in 1942 Other-Granny went to work, but lived for a while rent-free as caretaker for the manse. In 1946 she moved to a bedsit over a newsagents and, in lieu of rent, she rose at 4:30am to receive and sort the papers. Once she had sent the paperboys out she left for work in the offices at Waterloo Station. As soon as she got home she went to cook dinner for an elderly sea-captain and settle him for the night, and after that she did tailoring and mending as long as there was light. In the five years after Grandad died she managed to save enough.

The 'Making Mummy Happy' project was not working. She was angry. She said Granny had no right to buy 'Skeena'. She wasn't a Soal. She was a Jones. She had come from the gutter. And she'd no right to any part of Auntie Mary either.

I told Granny not to be upset and she said, 'Sticks and stones, may break your bones, but names can never hurt you.' and I should remember that.

Granny made sure we had fun despite the underlying tension and in between the rows we went to the beach, watched Punch and Judy, ate ice cream, and paddled in the sea.

Mummy said Granny could live with her sister and Daddy would buy Skeena for us. Daddy said he wouldn't. They rowed again. I think I'd got used to them being touchy, but it frightened Daniel and I hated the way it spoiled our day. It made us cry and they just got crosser. Might it be our fault somehow?

### *It's that pram again*

At Skeena, if everyone else was out, my mother bundled us into the pram and parked it round the end of the house, but since this put us outside Auntie Mary's front door, she would come and talk to us.

Auntie Mary's house was called Hazelton after a town on the Skeena River in NW British Columbia, where Auntie Lizzie went alone in 1902. She stayed more than twenty years teaching mixed-race girls in a culture where a man's life was worth a bottle of whisky; the price of hiring a killer.

If Auntie Lizzie was the family's answer to Annie Oakley, Auntie Mary was a sacred icon. She was a nurse when the profession was in its infancy, had cared for some exotic patients, including several monarchs, and travelled to places that would soon be closed to the west for fifty years. She was eighty that year but lived until I was fourteen. Strict but warm, and magical, it is an honour to have known her.

### *All change.*

The rollercoaster of joys and woes swooped on through August while my parents bickered, and Granny tried to convince Daniel and me we were having the time of our lives. Daddy played a lot of tennis, presumably needing to whack the hell out of something inanimate. Having a father around was a novelty. We watched him play, in his white shorts, jumper tied round his waist like a real sportsman.

Towards the end of August we visited a Mr and Mrs Busby in Ellis Road and Daddy bought their house. Just like that! Or so it seemed to us. The dark mood lifted and everyone was happy. We rode donkeys, and a miniature railway. We drank Cherryade and Vimto, (which I hated) and were allowed to paddle, in proper swimsuits knitted by Granny.

The beach to either side of Clacton Pier had been cleared of mines for a little way, though further on it was still blocked off with barbed wire and danger notices. Ships passed to and fro on the horizon, and we learned to recognise minesweepers by their shape.

We had our picture taken on the promenade by the same photographer as last year, and sitting on the same wall. How we had grown! Daniel had lost his baby look. We weren't so prim. My legs were longer and we looked like normal children who might just have some fun.

On 8th September (according to our IDs) we all went back to Birmingham to pack.

I have inherited an organising gene through my mother's line. Granny Soal spent time in service to families who moved entire households from town to country and back following the social season.

Through her my mother learned to move a family across England, supply clean clothes, beds and food on arrival and a sense of permanence within days. Packing up in Birmingham she was in her element.

I watched my mother folding and stacking and labeling, drawing plans of rooms, measuring, keeping notes. I wrote the names of the furniture on luggage tags for her, and she added the name of a room. We tied them to handles and knobs. Daddy spent hours in the garage.

### *Like Mistah Robison*

On Sunday's Daddy was on Church detail, and took us to the black meetings. Many of his old pupils from Jamaica were living in Birmingham and he wanted to say goodbye. There was a little girl called Winnie that I liked. She was learning to swim. I wanted to learn too because people said Winnie was half white. Now all the bits of Winnie I could see were definitely black, so I reckoned if I saw her in a swimsuit I'd see the white bits. Daddy said it didn't work like that.

I liked the black meetings. People talked to God properly, not in a sad whisper. They interrupted the preacher with encouraging shouts and no one seemed to mind. On our final visit they asked Daddy to sing.

'Like Mr Robeson,' they said. 'Hush we up! Mistah Eric gonna sing.'

He began, in his deep bass-baritone:
*'Were you there when they crucified my Lord?'*
For a moment all was quiet.
*'Oh! Oh! Sometimes I tremble, tremble, tremble.'*

Someone at the back said 'I'm tremblin' Lord!'

One or two voices agreed, but when my father began the second verse people started to hum. They hummed different notes that weren't the tune but sounded beautiful together. My skin tingled. Daniel's eyes were huge. It was our first experience of harmony and I think his love of choirs starts there.

Harmony, to Daniel, was something he wanted to be part of; to me it was the background to a soloist; and so our musical tastes diverged. Daniel spent his first two and a half years in a children's home as part of a group, while I had been alone. Perhaps that explains it.

### ***Floored.***

Despite my pleas to befriend Anthony Parsons, we'd not been allowed to play with other children, but in those last warm weeks of summer everyone was busy, and glad for us to be elsewhere. We went to Anthony's house preparing gooseberries for jam. He had a lisp and called me Livvitifith, which I liked. And we met a little girl called Eleanor who had moved in across the road.

Eleanor took us to see her rabbit. Her house was dark inside, with all the curtains drawn. Beyond the French doors the sun shone, but the house was deep in gloom. A thin woman sat curled in an armchair. We crossed the room. She did not speak. The floor was dark and polished but I was shocked at their poverty. There was no carpet, just a few dead animals strewn about the floor; a leopard complete with head, a zebra, and a nondescript brown thing with stripes at one end which hindsight suggests was an okapi.

'Mummy stays indoors,' Eleanor said as we examined the rabbit, 'She doesn't want people to see her cry.'

I sensed something was wrong but didn't like to ask.

I suggested we play at our house, but when we got there Mummy was out. She returned to find Eleanor and me dragging a kitchen chair up the steps to the lawn because I thought we'd have a picnic. I wasn't sure how, but was determined it would happen.

And it did. Mummy spread a cloth on the lawn and made us fish-paste sandwiches and orange-juice and found a few strawberries and raspberries in the garden. She told us later that Eleanor had lived in Africa, but her Daddy had been killed and they had to come back to England. To my surprise, I also learned that dead animals meant you were posh. Good! I had an owl.

The autumn term began, and on weekdays my father was back teaching sport at Handsworth Grammar School, where he had been both pupil and teacher. It was so much a part of him that it did not occur to me that he would have to leave.

### *Home is where?*

Our house was the only home I knew, but my father hardly knew it at all. War began soon after his marriage and for three years the house was rented out. In 1942 my mother and I moved in but Daddy had little chance to connect with it on his brief leaves from the RAF. Now he had been married eight years and his belongings were still at his parents' house. We spent time there packing his books.

Daddy's boyhood bedroom had a whole wall of books, floor to ceiling, and boxes of interesting things. We asked him about the humming at church and he said if you listened carefully you could hear other tunes behind the main one. He dragged a black box from beneath the bed. A gramophone.

'Listen to this.' he said, cranking the handle and placing the needle on the disc. It was "All In The April Evening" by the Glasgow Orpheus Choir. How did they *do* that?

Mummy also had black boxes; in the bottom of her wardrobe. One contained a human skull.

'This is Percy,' she said, showing me the way the bones held together like an exquisite jigsaw. 'He died young. He hadn't cut his wisdom teeth.'

And sure enough you could see them down in the bone of his jaw.

Bonfire night came and went. I wrote a new verse for my firework poem and Daddy told me that words like 'pop' and 'fizz' were called onomatopoeia, but you could put sounds into a poem using ordinary words too, if you found the right ones. He read me part of a poem about King Arthur where Bedivere in full armour carries him to the lake. 'the dint of armed heels' captivated me. Tennyson! I wanted to write like him.

### *The whole tooth.*

In the nursery, I stood on a chair and drew a tree on the blackboard wall as high as I could reach. I added leaves and flowers. I put branches lower down for Daniel. He drew cars on his. Mummy said cars didn't grow on trees and I said anything grew on ours. To prove it I replaced my flowers with chairs and saucepans and kittens.

Mummy said I was eccentric, like Daddy and Grandad. That was fine by me. I taught Daniel some letters. He used the chalk in his left hand so I did too. It was easier for him to copy. Apparently that was eccentric too.

There were tea chests everywhere, and trunks roped up with washing-line. Strange things appeared from cupboards, a device for making artificial cream, a coffee percolator. What was coffee? Something only posh people could have. Every drawer and shelf was empty. Only the nursery was untouched, but even there the lions' cupboard was bare.

There was fog outside and days grew cold, but Princess Elizabeth was getting married and people were excited. She would have a white dress and bridesmaids. I wished I could be one like I was for Cousin Reg.

One gloomy evening after dark I took it upon myself to fetch a glass biscuit jar from upstairs. The hall was dark with just a little light from a street-lamp outside. I tucked the jar under my arm, reaching up to the bannister with the other, and set off down the stairs, one careful step at a time. Half way down, I slipped. The jar tumbled glinting beside me and vanished into the darkness.

(*Don't cry. Stiff upper lip.*)

I sat on the bottom step. My upper lip didn't feel stiff, it felt sore and one of my front teeth felt odd. I touched it. It came away in my hand. That was it! I was finished! I had been careless and God had made me suddenly old. I would have false teeth in a glass, like Other-Granny. There would be no white dress for me. No bridesmaids. No babies. It was the END of the WORLD!

I sat clutching the tooth in my palm, staring out at the street lamp, the phone silhouetted against it like a big black daffodil, quiet tears breaking the light into rays. Oh no! I could hear Daddy's bicycle, a key in the lock...

'Hello!' he said, taking off his cycle clips, 'Why are you sitting here like Little Orphan Annie?'

I couldn't answer. He prised open my hand. I blurted my fears. Why was he laughing? He turned on the light and carried me to the mirror. I covered my face. I didn't want to see my white hair and wrinkled skin. Daddy made me look. I was fine. I was going to grow a whole new set of grown-up teeth, he said, better than the old ones. He picked up the jar, also undamaged, and we took it to the kitchen.

I never found out who Little Orphan Annie was but in bed at night I poked with my tongue and could just feel the rough edge of my new grown-up tooth.

### *House and home*

The pace quickened. The tea-chests disappeared. People came to look at the house and we had to keep it tidy. My mother washed our tree off the blackboard wall and Daniel was upset. I said we'd draw another one but he stamped on the chalks and they had to be thrown away.

The school inspector came again and Mummy said we were moving and it was none of his business. He said I'd missed a year of school and Mummy said she was a better teacher than any he knew. He went away. I would be starting school in Clacton anyway, so I concentrated on my writing. I made a short poem about squirrels and a longer one about an old lady that nobody visited. I wrote them out carefully in joined-up writing.

According to the Identity Cards we moved to Clacton on November 24th. We paid a last visit to the stables at Purus Bakeries. Some of the horses had known me all my life, and later I missed them most of all. I missed their smell, their warm sides, their big nostrils and heavy heads, their soft lips taking an apple from my palm. I missed the way they talked with their ears, or snorted into their nosebags blowing bran into my hair.

My memories of Birmingham have surprised me with their intensity and detail. I have lived in many places and wondered why this should be so immersive. Birmingham is not a place I would choose to live, but I recognise now that it formed me. I have watched myself take shape, my roots probing down into music and dance and books and wildlife and atoms and all my later passions. I can thank Birmingham at last, and recognise that it was home in a way I have not felt since.

# *Part Two*

# *Clacton-on-Sea*

# *Nine*

The Ellis Road house was not ready, so we lived at Skeena with Mummy while my father finished the school term in Birmingham. I was enrolled at the primary school in St Osyth Road and Granny came from London for my first week. I had a pleated tunic with a sash, and long warm stockings held up with suspenders that Mummy stitched to my liberty-bodice. Socks, she said, were common, and everyone would see that I came from a good family. Granny tutted and shook her head.

I was full of confidence that first day, and proud of being different. We spent the morning learning the rules; to stand when the teacher came in, not running in the corridors, and lining up in the playground when we heard the bell. Someone read a story. Lunch was gristly mince and lumpy potato, which I managed to eat, (*remembering the poor little children in Africa*). Then I needed the loo, a noisome cubicle on the far side of the playground. It was cold and dark with a draughty gap under the door.

I couldn't get my knickers down from under the suspenders. I undid the front ones but couldn't do them up again, and as I struggled the bell rang. I panicked. Knickers half up and stockings sagging down the front of my legs I hobbled across the playground in tears towards the lines of children waiting to march to class. They laughed. I grizzled. Somebody took me home.

Granny took me into town that afternoon with my clothing coupons. She bought me grey knee-socks and made elastic garters to stop them falling down. Mummy said Granny had made her look cheap and *she* had worn stockings at school. Granny said this wasn't 1922 and school would be all right tomorrow. It wasn't.

* * *

## *Writing wrong.*

St Osyth Road School was not like Cherry Orchard. The windows were high up, showing only grey sky. Great white globes hung on chains from lofty ceilings and I feared one might fall. The teacher was not the kindly Miss Baldwin, but a grim elderly woman in a grey cardigan and lace-up shoes

'Well, it's Lady Muck!' she said as I came through the door on Day Two.

(*Sticks and stones, I thought, Sticks and stones.)*

There was pencil and paper at each desk.

'Now let's see who can write their name at the top of the sheet.'

Carefully, I wrote "Elizabeth Innes" in my best longhand.

'What's this?' A ruler jabbed at my name. 'Are you trying to be clever?'

'Yes Miss,' I said, truthfully. (*After all it was what I was there for.*)

'Hold out your hand.' The ruler came down on my palm.

I froze with shock, my hand still out. The ruler came down again.

'Now, write your name again, please, in proper printing ... and your name is Mary.'

I said I was Elizabeth.

'The register says Mary. Now write.'

My right hand hurt, so because I could, I took the pencil in my left and started to print my name. The teacher snatched the pencil away and led me to the front of the class.

'This is Lady Muck who wants to run before she can walk,' she said 'What have you to say for yourself, Miss Clever?'

'Names can never hurt you.' I said, quoting Granny. (*Well, she did ask*).

She turned my left hand up, gave it three with the ruler, and sent me to my desk.

My hands still throbbed at teatime and I couldn't hold my fork. I confessed to being punished.

'WHAT!? ... HOW!?'

Suddenly Mummy and Granny were united, all bickering forgotten. Mummy, who didn't do hugs, grabbed me and held me tight to her chest while Granny fetched a cool cloth and witch-hazel for my swollen palms.

We all went to the school next day with Daniel in tow. There was an almighty row, which I enjoyed immensely and that was the end of that. It was almost the end of term anyway, so I stayed at home and my parents found Daniel and me places at Holland Road to start after Christmas.

It took a while to realise that when most people bought a house, they didn't keep the old one. I thought I would see Anthony Parsons and my new friend Eleanor soon. The school had made me miserable and I wanted to go home. Mummy explained that Clacton was home now and someone else was living in our old house. We were never going back. EVER! She also confirmed that I was Mary now, the first name on my birth certificate, and not Elizabeth, which was the second and chosen by someone else.

It was more than I could bear. Everything had gone, even my name. And my writing that I'd worked so hard at. That was wrong too. I had to go back to baby-letters. I took out my notebook in a passion and printed over my squirrel poem. I was so upset that the pencil broke.

Granny found me. 'Oh don't do that!' she said. 'Your writing is very good.'

'But I didn't write it. Elizabeth wrote it in Birmingham. I'm Mary now and Mary writes baby-letters.'

Granny shook her head in frustration. 'Well you'll always be Elizabeth to me.'

And so I was. For the next three years I was Elizabeth to my father and Granny Soal but Mary to everyone else.

### *Under the carpet.*

The Ellis Road house was ours, an empty shell now the Busbys had gone. Ancient carpets were ripped up ready for new lino. Daddy joined us at last and we were tasked with helping him remove the layers of old newspaper that lurked beneath. Newspapers. A mistake.

My father carried a sidetracking gene. It caused problems packing up in Birmingham when wrapping a model Spitfire turned into "Why aeroplanes stay up." complete with cross-sections of wings, arrows for lift and drag, and how many thousand feet you need to get a Spit out of a spin.

The Lino arrived at Ellis Road and was left in the hall because the three of us were still on our hands and knees in the dust while Daddy, pipe clamped in his teeth, read us the launch of the Queen Mary, and pointed out that Sherlock Holmes would deduce that the carpet had been laid after 1934. We would not move in by Christmas after all.

Meanwhile, looking to make local connections, my father checked out the Westcliffe Theatre at the far end of Ellis Road. There, on a dank dark evening, he met a comedian/impresario with a bad head cold, looking to stage a variety show. His name was Bunny Baron. Daddy invited him back to Skeena for hot toddy and sympathy. Thus he found a new friend, and Mummy found a new obsession. I had little to do with Bunny, but the members of his company "Sunshine and Smiles" were my mentors and child-minders for the next six years.

### *Age and beauty*

It was strange being with Other-Granny for Christmas instead of Granny coming to us, but it was the first of the four Clacton Christmases that formed my view of what Christmas should be and showed me how to organise it.

We made paper decorations in silver tape, and chains of coloured rings. Food was still rationed but Granny built a cottage from small slabs of cake and covered it with sweets. It was hollow and had windows with lights my father rigged up with a bicycle battery. Only posh people had turkey so we had a chicken, which was almost as unusual. There were linen napkins in rings. There were candles and silverware.

Great-great-Auntie Mary came from next door, and her sister Sarah who was in her eighties. They had hearing aids with black Bakelite microphones clipped to their dresses. I had never seen people so old. They sat us on the knees of their silky frocks. The folds of skin on their necks were soft. I thought they were beautiful, and have never feared old age. After lunch I played the RAF March on the piano for Daddy, with one finger and then the old ladies turned off their hearing aids and went to sleep.

Later we played 'Sorry' and 'Ludo' and there were Indoor Fireworks, things that squirmed about on the hearth or revealed invisible writing, and powders to throw in the fire that burned with coloured flames. Daniel and I distributed small gifts, delivered from a corner of the room by a big black spider that shot out on a wire set up by my mother.

Daniel had his first clockwork train, a single engine and carriage with a small oval of track. It was the start of a collection that we added to jointly once everyone realised I'd rather have a guard's van or a signal than a doll.

According to our ID cards we registered our move to Ellis Road on December 29th and although Granny was still registered in New Malden she was buying Skeena and her future was secure.

## *1948: Seeds of protest.*

Despite the winter weather Clacton seemed fresh and bright as 1948 began; new house, new school, new people, seeing more of Granny Soal. No longer 'Other-Granny', she became the only Granny as the Inneses faded into memory.

Although Granny did not move officially until the end of the year, she was at Skeena much of the time. Daniel and I were too, especially in the holidays, but 'home' was Ellis Rd.

23, Ellis Road was a four bedroom Edwardian semi. It had the usual front and rear receptions plus a family room at the end of the hall, which became the centre of operations. There were proper family breakfasts where Daddy read things from the paper and told us the news.

Mr Ghandi had stopped eating ... again ... which Mummy said didn't matter and Daddy said it mattered very much because Mr Ghandi was a Very Special Person.

But ... but ... You had to eat up your dinner or you might die, people said, and think of the starving children in Africa. I had seen pictures of Mr Ghandi and he looked far too thin already. I was distressed.

'Why won't he eat?' I wailed 'He'll starve to death.'

'It's called a protest,' Daddy said 'There are people who love Mr Ghandi all over the world, but the people who love him in India are fighting each other and if they're afraid of losing him, he thinks they might stop.'

'Jesus died to stop people fighting.' I said.

'Didn't work that time either.' muttered Daddy.

'ERIC!' Mummy's high horse took off at a canter. 'We need not concern ourselves with Mr Ghandi, children. He is a heathen of no consequence. You may leave the table.'

We obeyed.

My father took diary dictation from me that night. I always had more to say than my little hand could write. Could I stop eating, I wondered, to get what I wanted, or stop people quarrelling. I reckoned I was too fond of food, of scrambled eggs, of roast potatoes, rhubarb and custard, tripe and onions, everything in fact except blancmange and kippers ... and anyway, I was a mad Innes, and maybe nobody loved me enough to mind if I died.

'I do!' said Daddy interrupting 'Granny does!'

'Bother! I knew Daddy had to *listen* to my thoughts to write them down, but they were private and I didn't always want him to actually *notice* them.

### *Writing it right.*

After the disaster of St Osyth Road, the Holland Road School was a revelation, bright, warm, and welcoming. Classrooms led off the sides of the assembly hall, a polished parquet space with platform and high window at one end and doors at the other through which our lunches came to folding tables, set up each morning.

Daniel was four and a half and just starting school. Because his birthday was in September he went into Miss Weeks baby class. I would be six before the end of the school year and though there was only fourteen months between us I would always be two classes ahead.

I worried about my writing. Would I be in trouble again? That ruler really hurt. Mummy said it was all right.

'They don't hit at Holland Road. We don't want our hard work wasted, do we? So just do your best longhand and see what happens. If there's any trouble I'll be down to tell them what's what!'

She would too. I felt more confident. Mummy always knew what was what and wasn't afraid to say so.

* * *

I don't remember my teacher's name, a widow who was kind and smiley and read us tales of Sam Pig. We started the day writing simple sentences about our parents, occupations, sports, hobbies. I ignored the helpful words on the blackboard and wrote with great care :

*'My Daddy teaches jim (crossed out) gym and football and maths. He plays bowls.'*

I waited. My teacher looked at the paper closely.

'I think Miss Ault needs to see this.' she said.

Oh dear. Now I was for it!

Miss Ault was the headmistress and at playtime we went to her office.

'This is beautiful, Mary.' she said. (*Mary? I'd forgotten the name change.*) 'but I want you to do me a favour. You are very lucky to have someone to teach you joined-up writing, but the others can't do it yet, so while they are learning I'd like you to print to help them. Would you do that for me?'

'Have I got to write baby-letters then?'

'They're not baby-letters really. There are lots of ways of writing, but printing is easiest to start with. Keep practising longhand at home, but please be patient and print until the others can catch up.'

I was disappointed, but it made sense.

What were these other ways of writing, I wondered? My father dragged out a book of alphabets so beautiful I wanted to do them all. Then he showed us a Russian alphabet where P was R and H was N and Mummy said no wonder Russians were so dangerous.

As for my writing, I reverted to print at school but my heart wasn't in it, and at home, without supervision, my longhand became an irredeemable scrawl.

### *The world in black and white.*

It must have been a Saturday, not long afterwards, as Daddy was at home. Breakfast was long and late, and he was upset. Very upset. Someone had shot Mr Gandhi. Mr Gandhi was dead.

'But why? Who? I thought ...'

My father could not answer. He had no words. This big man was struggling. I thought Mummy might say something rude about Mr Gandhi but Daddy flashed her a warning look down the table.

'If you can't pull yourself together, Eric, you'd better go out. And you can take *them* with you.' Indicating us.

We walked down to the sea-front and sat on concrete steps by the beach. Daddy said nothing more about the shooting, but he talked about Gandhi's life, in India and South Africa. He pointed at the public loos and said that black people in South Africa couldn't use the same toilets as whites, or go to the same beach; and white people there wanted them all sent to live in the wilderness and only come to town to work.

'Like slaves!' I said, horrified. Daniel stared at the sea, too little to comprehend.

'Worse than slaves.' Daddy said.

We were Baptists so I knew about slaves in America, though I didn't know how they got there. I just knew they'd been freed ... so that was all right wasn't it? The truth was yet to come.

The sky was grey, the beach smooth and empty. The winter waves crashed in, hazy with sand and shreds of kelp. I couldn't take my eyes off the block of public loos.

Visiting Granny years later, as a young adult, the loos were still there. My daughter and I queued on the sand-strewn floor, midst the smell of carbolic and cold urine, and I remembered Gandhiji, and thought of the blacks of South Africa, still living under apartheid as my father had feared.

### *A growing conundrum*

The move from Birmingham to Clacton brought many new things into our lives, mostly because we were 'bigger'. This word was one of many linked to size and time, and the idea of 'growing'. I needed to sort them out. To know where I stood. I asked questions and scribbled my conclusions on an old paper bag. They went something like this ...

'Little' must be up to five,
... as we were 'little' in Birmingham.
Then you were 'Bigger' up to eleven when you became
... 'Big' and went to the 'big' school.
When you left school you were 'older'
... until you were twenty-one and became a 'grown-up'.
Grown-ups didn't get any bigger.
They were men and women until they got married.
Then they were Mummies and Daddies and then
... Grannies and Grandads
... and got a house with a billiard room.
Eventually they got a hearing aid and were called 'old'.

Sorted! I showed it to Daddy who laughed till he cried, told me I was a genius, and kept the paper-bag for the rest of his life.

### *In a word*

I got nine out of ten for my piece of writing, even though I didn't print, but my teacher said that 'maths' should have been 'mathematics'. I told my parents who said 'Oh really!' almost in unison, which was interesting.

I knew about mathematics, which was more than just sums. There were other bits that I couldn't do yet. There were squares and triangles and pi. I hoped it had apples in it, preferably with cloves. There was the square on the hyp ... hyp ... something or other. I knew that from Gilbert and Sullivan when Daddy sang the "Modern Major General". And there was algebra, which had puzzles where letters pretended to be numbers and you had to find out which. You didn't do that until big school. I could hardly wait.

The next school project was to choose a nursery rhyme at home, and write it out in class, asking our teacher the words we couldn't spell. I decided to practise at home.

'Twinkle, Twinkle ...' I wrote.

'No! No!' My father said. 'You'll need to use the proper words at school.' He wrote it out for me. I practised, unaware that he was sending my teacher up.

'Scintillate, scintillate,' I wrote next day 'globule ...' I couldn't remember the rest.

‘What's this?’ said my teacher.

‘It's the proper words, Miss; not using the easy ones, like 'maths'. Daddy wrote it out for me. He's got a thesaurus.’ I fished his crumpled paper from my pocket. She read it ...

*Scintillate, scintillate, globule vivivic!*
*Fain would I fathom thy nature specific*
*Loftily poised in the ether capacious*
*Strongly resembling a gem carbonaceous.*

‘Somebody,’ she said, ‘needs to have words with your Daddy.’

I spent three years plus one term at Holland Road School, longer than at any other, and although I remember the playground, the food, and events in the assembly hall, I have no recollection after the first weeks, of teachers, lessons or classrooms until almost the end in 1951. I was given little projects and left to do them alone while the others worked through things I had done long ago. I arrived at five with the basic education of a ten-year-old. Perhaps they didn't know what to do with me.

Often, I was sent with messages to other classrooms across the assembly hall. Briefly the great shiny herringboned floor was all mine and I crossed it like a ballerina, pirouette, jettė, pas de chat, curtsey.

I do remember 'Music and Movement' in that hall, to the Schools Radio Programme. ‘Find a space.’ the presenter said, and we stretched like cats, picked imaginary flowers, or turned slowly like windmills. Occasionally we learned a dance, like Gay Gordons, or the Veleta, and I got to hold hands with another child for a precious moment.

Most of all I remember Miss Ault, the headmistress because, in my darkest hour, she remembered that, for all my sophistication, I was still a little girl, and needed a hug.

# Ten

The Making Mummy Happy project went into overdrive. Outwardly my parents became a golden couple. My father signed them up for the CADS (Clacton Amateur Dramatics Society), the Operatic Society, The Caledonian Society, and supporters of the Pier, the Westcliffe Theatre, and of course, the Carnival.

I was enrolled with Joan Thorogood's Dance School, the Baptist Sunday School, and the cadets of the Girls' Life Brigade, which had a smart navy uniform with a red trim and a sailor collar.

My parents fitted kiddy-seats to their bicycles and we went to Walton-on-the-Naze and found curly fossils in the cliffs. The coast went on forever, and I wondered how far you could get if you kept walking. France probably.

More mines were cleared from the beaches and Daddy hired us a beach hut near Clacton Pier. It was a small white one on the east side and quite beneath Mummy who complained bitterly until the following year when we qualified for a posh one to the west. Meanwhile the beach got busier, the weather got warmer, and the flowerbeds broke out in wallflowers on the promenade.

As she had in Birmingham Mummy knocked down our front wall and planted a rockery that spilled onto the footpath. The wall was full of ants and we watched them carrying their eggs to safety as we removed the bricks. She painted "Wyndcliffe" on the glass transom over the door, in ornate letters, in memory of her childhood home in Somerset.

And Mummy did seem happy for a while, happier than I saw her before or afterwards. We had a lot of fun that summer and I felt we were a real family like the ones on the wireless or the Giles Family in the paper. We had the Express because Mummy wouldn't let the Herald over the doorstep. Not even to light the fire, she said. Daddy sometimes left one in the kitchen on purpose and Mummy screamed as if she'd seen a spider and carried it to the dustbin with tongs.

Yes, an ordinary, slightly wacky, family. But we weren't. Not even close.

### *Passing Strangers*

So who were these people, Win and Eric, struggling their way into a dazed Britain after years apart? Thousands of other couples made it, so what went wrong?

I know now that my mother had obsessions and extremes of fantasy from childhood, confused further by Calvinist dogma. She married in August 1939 and within weeks war was declared and Eric was gone. Pregnant in 1942, in a world gone mad, she lost her beloved father weeks before my birth, and lived out the war among her in-laws in Birmingham. Fleeing to Clacton, she found herself now, with a full-time husband, two children, and no way to use her teaching qualifications or acting skills. She was 32. Even the most stable person would have struggled, but stable she was not.

My mother was a perfectionist, my father an idealist. His education drew him away from rigid paternalism. As a young man teaching in Jamaica, he declared that black people didn't need to be guided. They needed to be equal. Women, too, must be acknowledged, and everyone should be free to succeed. He was years ahead of his time. Birmingham University and teacher training in Glasgow broadened his mind further, and distanced him from his family. Now, after a war and seven years in the RAF he longed for an ideal world of cosy families and fulfilled career women; an impossible dream. He had been married nine years. He was almost forty. And he was living with a woman he hardly knew.

### *A room of ones own.*

My mother worked her magic on Ellis Road, with speed and precision. She scraped and smoothed and varnished. She ordered glass. She filled and puttied. She sized and papered. Sometimes we stayed with Granny Soal away from the paint fumes. Daddy was no good at that sort of thing and knew to stay out of the way. Mummy was in her element and it's a wonder the sewing machine didn't give off smoke.

The front room became our playroom, its old Lino brightened with floor-paint; a room to dance in, and for plasticine and crayons and glue and lovely messy things. The room behind it was a locked parlour where we could not go, but life mostly happened in the family room and kitchens at the end of the hall where the wireless kept up a stream of music and plays and news, and such food as rations allowed was eked out with home-grown veg.

To either side of the master bedroom, Daniel and I had rooms of our own, and between them my mother recreated the glamourous art-deco boudoir from Birmingham, with its great round mirror and silky coverlet. One look at that and Ellis Road felt like home at last ... and bigger. Daddy even had a room of his own and didn't have to share. I never imagined it was unusual.

At the back of the house, down a corridor, beyond the bathroom, my father's room had a bed, a desk, the walls of books, and the red 'turkey' carpet from his parents' house. We were allowed just inside the door to access the first rank of bookcases. There he assembled our reference toolkit; dictionary, thesaurus, The Children's Encyclopedia, and more and he showed us how to use it.

On higher shelves, out of our reach were books to use under supervision; Fowler's English Usage, a dictionary of Phrase and Fable, and another of quotations, a complete Shakespeare and a Bible concordance. They held the answers to a million questions.

At weekends with the dictionary to hand, Daddy turned rhymes and proverbs into 'real' words. I don't remember all of "The Domiciliary Edifice Erected by John" but it taught us what feline, canine and bovine meant. A crumpled horn was a 'corrugated protuberance' and a kiss an 'osculatory gesture'. Best of all was 'the reverend ecclesiast whose cranium was devoid of all hirsute appendage.' I tried it out on friends at school, but they didn't get it at all.

* * *

## *The One and only*

I missed Birmingham for a while, the bakery horses, the town centre skies black with starlings in winter dusk, the trams, Grannie and Grandad. I realised that they were far away now. Daddy visited them when we could afford his fare. I did not know that I would see them only three or four times more. They were my family. They loved me didn't they? I thought they would always be there.

Granny Soal was the only Granny now. No longer Other-Granny, she was just streets away, and hands-on in a way Grannie Innes never was. She cooked and sewed. She could do baths and wash hair. And she had a box of games that kept us enthralled for hours.

With all their social involvements my parents were often out at night. Granny baby-sat in term-time, or we were wheeled down to Skeena in the pram to stay with her.

We were always there at weekends and Granny knitted us swimsuits and let us play outside in them, even though Skeena was a mile from the sea.

The tooth-fairy lived at Skeena too, but never visited Ellis Road, so I saved my teeth for her as they fell out one by one, and like Granny, she never let me down. I thought it might be nice to live with Granny all the time, but she didn't have enough books.

Although I last saw Skeena when I was twenty-three, the house remained in the family until I was in my forties, and in my exile, at least I knew it was *there*. As a child, and a young adult, through all the changes of places and schools and custodies, it remained, firm, like an iron ring in a harbour wall. I could lash my storm-tossed heart to it while Granny piped me ashore.

## *All done with mirrors.*

We were always wheeled to Skeena in the pram, and whenever Mummy turned up and found us playing, she whisked us into it, and Granny whisked us out again at once. They had words.

One day, pushing a garden cane down the path, it caught on a stone and the near end jabbed my thigh. I doubled over.

Mummy grabbed me, shaking so hard I thought my head would fall off. 'Silly little fool!' she hissed 'No one will marry you now.'

'Don't be ridiculous, Win!' Granny said, snatching me away and uncovering a small wound on my leg.

'It's their wickedness,' said Mummy, 'They can't be trusted to play.'

Granny said 'Hrumph!' in a way that made her neck wobble, and popped a plaster on my leg.

'It's best she doesn't marry anyway,' said Mummy, 'We don't want any more mad Inneses.'

But I *had* to marry *somebody* when I grew up. I was a girl. What else was there to do? Granny said I would be fine and I'd have a white dress like Princess Elizabeth, and she'd make it for me, God willing, so that was all right.

Patchy was back, the black and white kitten bought for Mummy last year, except he was a cat now, and certainly wasn't the same Patchy we had in Birmingham. His white bits were in different places. I didn't ask.

We got a tortoise in May, which fascinated the cat but terrified Daniel who screamed when it hid in its shell. Mummy said he was a sissy. His stammer was worse since he went to school and Mummy declared that a shock might cure him.

'Like hiccups.' she said, and took us down to the pier.

Plan A was to ride Steel Stella, the roller coaster. I was terrified and have not ridden a roller coaster since, but Daniel loved it, so for Plan B, Mummy took him into the hall of mirrors and left him there.

Out on the pier we could hear him screaming.

'He's only four, for goodness sake!' Granny yelled, 'Do something!' Mummy stalked off.

I dashed back in and found him quite quickly. 'You follow the floor-boards,' I told Granny, 'The mirrors are a trick.'

We found Mummy at the shooting range knocking heck out of a row of tin ducks. I wondered if she might shoot me but she ignored us so we went to find a dish of cockles instead. But I felt angry ... and afraid. Something wasn't right.

## *Men and myth*

Among the things we had now we were 'bigger' were comics. We quickly outgrew Tiny Tots and Chicks' Own and moved on to Film Fun and Mickey Mouse Weekly. Daddy didn't allow The Beano or The Dandy as they encouraged you to laugh at other people's misfortunes, but other children had them at school.

Except for the front page, boys' comics were black and white, with red highlights, and had adventure stories about the Foreign Legion or white hunters in pith helmets being boiled in pots by black men with bones through their noses.

I guessed these were pretend creatures like Martians and unicorns and only meant for play. They were known as 'natives' or 'da*kies' and were nothing to do with the real people of Birmingham and Jamaica ... were they? So they featured in our games.

We couldn't mix with people near our hut east of the pier, Mummy said, as they were common. Daddy got angry. He even kicked the pram. He said we needed to run about, and walked us west of the pier to race on the prom. Sometimes we went so far that we couldn't see him. We felt very brave.

There were no black people in Clacton which seemed strange after Birmingham, but one day, up towards Butlin's, looking for monsters, we saw one, a tall man in a pale suit and Panama hat. He was part of the scenery, part of the game.

'A da*kie!' yelled Daniel, and we raced back down the prom squealing and giggling. 'A da*kie! A da*kie!'

'*A WHAT?!!*' Daddy leapt to his feet.

'A da*kie!' We gasped, out of breath, 'but we got away.'

'*DID HE HEAR YOU?*' Daddy was shouting. 'Take me to where he is! You will apologise!'

Holding us firmly by the wrists he propelled us back down the prom. Daniel was too little. I knew it was down to me. I was mortified. I should have thought. And what would an angry black man be like? An angry Daddy was bad enough.

I stood in front of the man, a dark silhouette against the bright sky. Daddy introduced himself. The man was from Jamaica. Daddy said something in patois. They laughed.

'My daughter has something to say to you.' Daddy said.

'I'm most terribly sorry.' I said in my politest voice.

'Hmmm!' said the man, 'Can you say that Jamaica way?'

I looked at Daddy. He whispered something in my ear.

'Mi sarry mistah.' I said

A big pink hole opened up in the round black face and the man threw his head back and laughed. Daddy arranged to meet him for a beer and we set off back to the hut. On the way the photograph-man snapped us, and Daddy ordered a copy. We look most contrite. We promised not to call anyone da*kie again.

'Is it like laughing at other people's misfortune?' I asked.

Daddy said, 'A bit.'

'But why is it a misfortune to be black?'

'It's a long story.' but he said no more.

### *Questions of policy*

I knew nothing of parties or politics. I did know we had a Prime Minister who, along with the King, was in charge of everything. Mr Atlee had taken over from Mr Churchill, and had stolen all the trains, or so Mummy said over tea. He would run them into the ground, she said, and she'd have to travel Third Class with the hoi-poloi.

'You do anyway,' said Daddy. 'Nobody travels First Class on my salary.'

'There are ways and means.' said Mummy mysteriously.

And now Granny had new glasses, free, from the government. A handout, said Mummy. That was how low she had sunk. Daddy said it was a grand idea and Mummy called him a socialist.

'Well at least we won't have to pay for her teeth.' she added.

'Your mother's always paid for her own teeth,' Daddy said 'It's yours I have to fork out for.'

He had just fallen through some very thin ice. Mummy had a partial upper denture, but we weren't supposed to know.

'There was nothing wrong with my teeth. That's show-business. You have to have some teeth out to define your cheek-bones and then use false ones when you eat.'

I didn't fancy that idea at all. I would soon be six and was slowly getting my grown-up teeth. Maybe I could keep them if I only wanted to sing and dance. I didn't want to act. I said so.

'You'll do what your agent tells you,' said Mummy, 'and to start with that will be me.'

I threw a tantrum and was sent to bed. Mr Atlee was welcome to the trains, but nobody was taking bits off my body. It was mine!

# Eleven

I was six on the 10th of July and Daddy was forty soon afterwards. Bedtime stories became more serious. I had my own books, of course, "Little Grey Rabbit", "The Faraway Tree", and "The Famous Five", but bedtime was for Daddy's books.

He read us "Uncle Remus" and told us more of slavery, and people being bought like horses and dogs. We asked questions but there were sad, cruel things behind the stories that we were too young to know, Daddy said, so we didn't want to hear about Brer Rabbit any more. It felt uncomfortable.

Instead we had Kipling's "Just So Stories". There was a whole row of Kiplings in Daddy's room, bound in burgundy leather with gold letters. We learned to find the Limpopo River on a map, and why 'fever-trees' were so called. There were Ethiopians, djinns and Parsees, and Yellow Dog Dingo chasing Old Man Kangaroo through the spinifex. We looked them all up in the Children's Encyclopedia. We learned the poems and tried to avoid 'camelius hump, the hump that is black and blue.' though people were getting the hump more often in our house it seemed.

### *School's out!*

Spring turned to summer and although it was school during the week we spent weekends at the beach. If Daddy was there, or Granny was in charge we could play and at the end of the day we helped the deck-chair man fold the chairs and get them up onto the prom. There were no health and safety concerns. You only trap your finger in a deck-chair once.

I remember that summer as long and sunny. My parents were much involved with the carnival, dressing floats and stalls, and organising sports, so Granny had charge of us down by the beach hut, and although the pram came in handy at meal times, there were hours of play.

And Granny played too. She tied my hair back from my face and let us run about in our undies. She rolled off her stockings and walked in the sand. She helped to build castles. And she tucked up her dress and paddled. We made patterns with footprints at low tide and popped the bubbles of bladder wrack. Tiny crabs ran over our fingers or buried themselves in a flash, and ragworms left casts at the tide's edge.

We were cleaned up and neatly dressed before Mummy saw us, but she knew because our backs and chests were brown. We had become 'street Arabs' but it was too late. We had learned to have fun.

There was fresh air and sunshine. We grew. For a third year we posed for the photographer, sitting on our usual wall. The plump little legs of 1946 were two years older, longer, slimmer. Daniel had lost his baby look and our hair was thick and strong. We posed with armfuls of peppermint rock, a prop representing weeks of rations. It would be six more years before we could buy them without coupons.

The jolly London relations came down for Carnival, an assortment of great-aunts in stout shoes, who sat on the beach in overcoats for fear of the sea breeze. On the warmest days they shed their coats and dozed in deck-chairs, faces protected by handkerchiefs secured under the brims of their pre-war hats. They did not paddle or play in the sand but they gave good cuddles, taught me to play cats-cradle, and carried a weary Daniel for miles on their backs.

This was my first carnival and the preparation proved as exciting as the event. Daddy pored over books illustrating divers and swimmers and elaborate pyramids of gymnasts, while, my mother sewed costumes for the carnival parade. People arrived at Ellis Road for fittings and all manner of bizarre costumes hung round the playroom picture rail.

Clothes were still rationed and fabric hard to find but there were old sheets and black-out curtains so Mummy made me a nun's habit, with a white wimple that tied on top of my head and a starched cap to hold up my veil.

Carnival came and we rushed daily from place to place, applauding and supporting. My parents seemed to know everyone and were sought out when things went wrong.

Daddy played water-polo and judged a diving contest. There were talent contests, dance displays, and demonstrations of field-sports. Daddy threw shot and javelin. Daniel and I spent hours looking for straight sticks to throw, and Mummy wisely locked the garden canes in the shed.

On the day of the parade I wore my nun's habit and rattled my collecting tin at the crowd. We walked behind the glamorous floats of the Westcliffe Theatre, and the company of the "Sunshine and Smiles" variety show, who let me ride when my legs got tired.

I had never known such excitement. Most exotic of all was Mummy, in her Indian outfit, all silk and embroidery, her arms hung with bangles, and an earthenware pot on her head. To me she was the most beautiful woman in the world.

Other people thought so too, and she was *my* Mummy. I felt very lucky ... and guilty ... and I promised God I would love her and be good. I didn't know how hard that would be.

### *A need to breathe*

When the relatives returned to London, Granny went with them for a break and the terrible pram reappeared. Daddy was planning lesson schedules and sports fixtures, so Mummy was in charge of us at the beach.

It was late August. The crowds were thinning out and there was more room on the sand, but we were still in the pram, as we were all summer unless Granny rescued us. We weren't strapped in as we had been in Birmingham, but we knew better than to get out.

In the afternoons the hood was up and a tartan rug thrown over like a tent. It was suffocatingly hot. We sat facing each other across the tray in the stifling dark and sometimes tried to sleep, resting our heads on our arms. We whispered. 'I'm thirsty.' or 'I wish Granny would come.' We could hear other children and tried to guess what they were doing, and we learned to play 'pat-a-cake' in complete silence.

We hated it. I protested sometimes but Daniel was too little and afraid to complain. Mummy needed time to read her magazine, she said, or talk to other grown-ups. I tried to understand, but the urge to resist was taking hold.

Adventure! That's what we needed, my brother and I. Children in stories had adventures. They made decisions, got themselves and adults out of danger, and returned home to relieved parents and grateful policemen. My birthday book was “Five Go To Smugglers Top” so Enid Blyton takes some of the blame for what happened next.

Like The Famous Five we needed to prove ourselves, I reckoned; to prove we could be trusted on our own and out of the pram. I decided that if we walked far enough along the beach we should get to France and if no one else was interested I'd have to arrange it myself.

Getting us up very early I checked we were properly dressed, combed Daniel's hair and wrote a note.

*‘We have gone on a pich-nich.*
*I have given Daniel a strate parting.’*

The parting was important. It's accuracy showed that you were 'fit to be seen', and I wanted Mummy to be proud of us, not ashamed.

‘Where are we going?’ Daniel asked, his little legs hurrying beside me.

‘To France.’ I replied, as we turned left at the pier and set out along the sand.

It was quite a slog and we had to scramble off the beach now and then due to barbed wire, and notices that said:

**"DANGER! MINES!"**

There was hardly anyone about. Up on the road I found a shop open and bought pop and a penny Hovis loaf with my pocket money. I don't remember how far we got or who took us home, but I was disappointed to learn that you couldn't get to France on foot via Walton-on-the-Naze.

### ***Coupons and costumes.***

Deliverance came with the return of Granny Soal and the purchase of a real swim-suit. It was late in the season. The price was reduced and it only needed one clothing coupon. There were two colours, red and navy, and I wanted a red one badly. I fixed my eyes on the navy one so that Mummy thought I wanted it. She bought the red.

'It's a waste,' she said to Granny who had donated the coupon. 'She can't learn to swim. She might have a seizure.'

'She doesn't have seizures.' said Granny.

'It's only a matter of time. She's an Innes. It's in the blood.'

She always said that. Perhaps I should be careful not to bleed in case I passed it on.

Summer was ending, and with Granny around we got to play again. She bought us spades.

I haunted the water's edge alone, the beach almost deserted. At low tide Granny was a distant figure, knitting in her deck-chair while Daniel made sand-pies at her feet. I built low walls around myself, flimsy bastions against the incoming tide. Within their circles, briefly, I felt safe and free. Perhaps the friendly waves would wash me flat with the sand, and God could draw a new little girl that Mummy liked.

He didn't. And I never learned to swim either, physically or emotionally. When the big waves roll in I take a deep breath and wait to see where I wash up.

Granny was knitting our winter woollies, unraveling old garments, washing the wool and weighting the skeins as they dried, to straighten out the kinks. Nothing was wasted. Even the shortest strands were carefully knotted together before we held the wool for her to wind it.

Clothes were not just rationed, but expensive. Daniel's new trousers were bought two sizes too big, pulled up under his armpits and safety-pinned to his shirt. Old garments were unpicked and remade some with delicate fabrics from before the war. Granny made herself dresses and donated her coupons for us. And then Mummy went to London and came home in a fabulous new coat.

Where had she got it? Who paid for it? She refused to say. And the coupons? She had used Granny's, and ours along with her own. She said it didn't matter because rationing would end soon. There was trouble, but in an odd way it was good to see something stylish and new, and Granny said we could *all* enjoy seeing it except Mummy who was wearing it. Maybe rationing *would* end soon.

My mother's new coat was indeed spectacular. Not in colour or trim, but in line and cut. It was black, with a nipped in waist, a wide skirt with big patch pockets and a round collar that spread across her shoulders. It was the New Look, not the exaggerated shape of Dior's fashion pictures, but wearable and shapely. Granny worried that it might be illegal as there were restrictions on design, but the fashion-police stayed away.

We had mice again. Pet mice. Around Whitsun my mother had dusted off the glass-fronted case and bought a black-and-tan buck and a white doe, naming them Rex and Blanche. There was no plan. She just popped them into their quarters and left them to it ... whatever 'IT' was. Within weeks there were dozens of them, mostly multicoloured like tortoiseshell cats. How this came about was a mystery. Granny said it was arranged by God, who 'worked in mysterious ways'.

There were no little harnesses or training sessions as there had been with the Birmingham mice, but Patchy sat by the case, as Peter had done, chattering his teeth and twitching while the mice jeered through the glass.

Mummy sold a box full of mice to the pet shop and bought a second case and another pair, Pearl who was silver-grey and Ginger who was ... well ... ginger. He was a bully and Pearl would have nothing to do with him. Mummy sent Blanche in to sort him out and Pearl settled in happily with Rex. Daddy made jokes about wife-swapping that we didn't understand.

Mummy was still taking surplus mice to the pet shop in Jackson Road. Blanch and Ginger occasionally produced plain white ones, which they particularly wanted. We used to carry them in a box but now she had the coat she just popped them in her pocket.

One morning, we met a neighbour and stopped to chat. I stood quietly by. A mouse ran up from the coat pocket and disappeared under the collar, quickly followed by another.

Mummy carried on chatting, though I'm sure she knew. I just watched the other woman who was trying to act normally and staring at the collar while two pink tails dangled from beneath. The woman excused herself quite quickly and Mummy swept her hand up under her collar and popped the mice back into her pocket.

### *That's entertainment!*

At the Westcliff Theatre, "Sunshine and Smiles" were packing costumes and scenery for storage. My mother had haunted the theatre all summer and made many friends in the company. There were tearful goodbyes. We went in search of Bunny Baron, the top man. He had gone. Mummy was upset. Why would he say farewell to my father and not to her. *She* was the true thespian. Daddy had no right etc. etc.

Mummy soon calmed down. The show would be back next spring and meanwhile CADS went into rehearsal for their next production. I don't recall the name of the play but I do remember my balding father wearing a ginger periwig and false paunch, so something Restoration I would guess. Daddy with hair! Gosh! My hair, however, was a mess; too straight, Mummy declared. Granny agreed.

In a doomed attempt to turn me from an urchin to a young lady they used curling tongs, an instrument of hair-torture that I despised. I had perfect manners. I did not need curls to be genteel. But Granny liked curls too, and I fought a battle for the next decade, escaping eventually with my follicles intact.

We rolled into autumn rehearsing for plays, pantomimes, nativities, carol services, and a dance school concert. I played a powder-puff on a magic dressing-table. Once more the house was full of costumes and Mummy was kind and happy.

As she sewed we listened to Woman's Hour, Mrs Dale's Diary, or Housewives Choice. Noel Coward sang "Dance Little Lady" and I promised him I would. Woman's Hour serialised "The History of Mr Polly", and I danced my way to and from Miss Thorogood's to the signature tune "Jumping Bean".

Winter was coming. On Armistice Day, as the littlest cadet in the GLB, I wore a harness and carried a flag into

Pier Avenue Baptist Church. We found the tortoise digging a hole in the compost heap, and put him to bed in a straw-filled tea-chest in the shed. Mummy took all the mice to the pet shop and traded them in for a second cat. And Princess Elizabeth had a baby and called him Charles.

### *It's official.*

Skeena belonged to Granny at last. Moving slowly through a legal system overloaded with unfinished business from before the war, the executors of the two linked wills finally sorted out the loose ends. Granny's ID card shows her officially registered there on November 4th 1948.

My mother was still angry that Skeena was not hers. She was rude about double-great-uncle Ernie for allowing the sale and told people he sold fake antiques, made by his nephew Willie Payne who even faked the worm-holes. I didn't believe her.

We had Christmas at Skeena and Granny iced the cake as two little children in a double bed surrounded by marzipan toys. The double-great-aunties came as before and were gently escorted home to bed in the late afternoon after Daniel and I, dressed as pixies, produced gifts from a giant mushroom made of cardboard and a waste-paper basket. Our parents walked back to Ellis Road later, but we stayed with Granny for two more nights ... to help her finish the trifle.

### *1949: The Joyce Grenfell effect.*

We had lived in Clacton for a year, enjoying our playroom at the front of the house. We had a double easel for painting, Meccano, picture dominoes, and plasticine, but after my attempt to walk to France along the beach, all that stopped. Having a bright idea on my own was another sign of madness, Mummy said. Daniel and I must be separated, and play on our own in our rooms. The playroom was out of bounds, and besides, she had other plans for it. She was opening a school.

There were deliveries of equipment, blackboards, chalks, wooden beads for threading, triangles and tambourines, tubs of powder-paints, little aprons, stacking-tables and chairs.

By Easter, seventeen three and four year olds were signed up, and two rows of low-level coat-pegs adorned the wall at the foot of the stairs, each identified by a picture.

The coats that hung upon these pegs were all brand new. Clothes rationing had indeed ended and the parents of the children were in serious competition. This was not child-care for working Mums, but for women needing time for hairdressers and dress-makers, and having coffee with their friends. Before the war these families would have had nannies but social structure was changing, as were budgets, and nursery schools were the answer, the more prestigious the better.

There was kudos in getting your child in with my mother. After all, Mrs Innes and her husband were on every committee in sight. She was a parson's daughter and great-niece of Lizzie Soal the missionary, and Mary who had nursed kings.

Teacher training changes and evolves. I don't think my mother was more than a Certificated Teacher, but she was very good at it. She had a charisma that made people want to please. It was all such fun you hardly knew you were learning.

Most married women were banned from teaching until 1944, though I've never been sure whether my mother was a teacher who wanted to act, or an actress who wanted to teach. I suspect the latter. She certainly put on a performance.

She was a fan of Joyce Grenfell and affected a singsong nursery-teacher tone, ramping up the upper-class vowels. Yes, I know I do it too, though I'm more Dame Maggie Smith. It comes in handy sometimes.

# *Twelve*

Now that Mummy had her school it was, she said, most important that we were perfectly behaved outside the house, so that no one should know about my madness. Daniel, too, was a child of Satan, though Mummy wouldn't explain why. God had sent us to her because He knew she would stop us harming anyone, and of course, she loved us very much, even if no one else could, and even though we would have to go to hell in the end. I felt sad for her and wished she could have had nice children like other people. I promised myself I would try to be good.

When we adopted Daniel I looked forward to a little brother. Now I was a 'lonely only' again, as was he, writing and colouring alone in our rooms. We saw each other at meal times, in the bath, in the queue for the school bus, and to listen to Children's Hour, otherwise we had to wait to visit Granny, a few streets away, who treated us as if we were normal.

Granny took us to Marks and Spencer's for our new couponless clothes. There were snug-fitting vests and knickers in white 'interlock' that looked like tiny knitting, and Wincyette pyjamas. There were warm grey knee-socks with coloured bands round the top and everything had St Michael or St Margaret on the label.

You didn't help yourself in M&S. There were girls behind each counter who asked what you wanted, and what size, and found it for you. Sometimes they came out with a tape and measured you.

### *Changing the world*

We didn't see much of Daddy in term-time. He taught in Colchester, left the house before we did, and came home at bedtime. Children's Hour finished at six.. We undressed for bed while he listened to the news and if we were lucky he would read to us or, even better, he would sing.

Silhouetted against the light on the landing Daddy stood framed in my doorway, or Daniel's and sang of Jock of Hazeldene, or Danny Boy, Leezy Lindsay or the Lassie wi' the Yellow Coatie.

Sometimes there was a story and a song to go with it. He told us how all the potatoes died in Ireland and people went to live in America, and he sang The Praties They Grow Small. I learned them all and sang them silently inside my head whenever I was bored or unhappy, or on nights when the madness made him cross and he shut himself in his room.

As Spring arrived breakfasts moved from porridge to cornflakes, and at weekends, new exotic cereals; Weetabix or Shredded Wheat, but still with hot milk until the weather was warmer. Daddy was home at weekends too, outside, tinkering with bicycles and lawn mowers.

Mummy was happy. She had her school, a place in the community, and new clothes. "Sunshine and Smiles" returned to the Westcliffe Theatre for the summer season, and Mummy sang all around the house, "I'm Going to See You Today" which was Joyce Grenfell's hit song, and she unpacked her crystal-ware at last and arranged it on the dresser.

We weren't allowed to throw balls in the kitchen because of the crystal-ware, but I had a woolen pom-pom made by Granny, that hung long ago in my pram, multicoloured and of every sort of wool. I examined it minutely, 'befriending' my favourite strands, or bounced it gently in my hand. At night it went under my pillow.

I was sitting behind the kitchen door, gently lobbing the pom-pom from palm to palm, when Mummy walked in and snatched it away.

'No throwing in the kitchen!' she said and flung it into the fire.

I tried to run but she caught my shoulders and made me watch as the beautiful colours writhed and turned grey on the coals. There was a dreadful smell. I dashed outside and shut myself in the shed.

'What's going on?' It was Daddy. I told him.

'Well, it depends how you define throwing,' he said, 'but you took a risk and it didn't pay off. You'll need to put it behind you.'

'But I'll never get it back,' I sobbed

'No ... No, you won't. But we can't keep everything forever, you know. We have to make room for the future, else we won't have time to change the world.'

'But I'm too little to change the world.'

'Just presently, but you never know, and anyway you don't have to be Tarzan to make a difference.'

And he told me how Queen Elizabeth sat on her horse and told the soldiers she had a woman's body but a man's heart. I liked that. Afterwards we found the tortoise waking up, rustling in his straw, and I was distracted from my tears.

Later I stood at my wardrobe mirror, with my clenched fist over my heart.

'I may have the weak and feeble body of ... er ... somebody who's six,' I said, 'but I have the heart and stomach of ...'

(*Think of a hero. Oh, I know ...*)

'Dick Barton, Special Agent!'

### *Perambulation.*

Another thing making Mummy happy was acquiring an up-market terraced beach hut to the west of the pier. These were substantial huts with double-doors and verandas, perched slightly above the promenade. One fine morning in late May, with a few hours before lunch with Granny, we opened it up for the first time. Daddy went down ahead of us, and Mummy dragged out the pram. Our hearts sank.

We were five and six. Our legs were too long for the pram now. Even in its deep belly with feet tucked backward under the seat, my knees knocked bone on bone against Daniel's's as Mummy trundled us down to the sea. Surely we weren't going to spend another summer of heat and cramp watching other children play.

The hut doors were open wide, but Daddy was not smiling.

'Why would you want to be seen west of the pier with that scruffy old tub?' he asked.

Mummy said he'd need to buy her a decent one then.

‘They don't *need* a pram.’ said Daddy

‘Of course they do. How else am I to restrain them?’

‘They are children, Win, not rattlesnakes.’

Mummy grabbed the haversack of towels and slung it on her shoulder. ‘They were your wretched idea, so you can wheel them down to Mother's. I'm taking a taxi.’ and she swept off up the prom.

I wanted to know what she meant, but Daddy wouldn't say. He locked up the hut and set off for Granny's, trying to make it a joke. It was about a mile. Part way down St Osyth Road he stopped on a corner.

‘Let's say hello to this horse.’ he said, lifting us from the pram and rubbing our numb legs.

The horse was attached to a cart a little way down a side-street and while we were saying hello, Daddy was loading the pram onto the cart with the rag-and-bone man.

‘We're walking the rest of the way,’ he said, ‘and how do we get there? We Follow the Yellow Brick Road.’ and he set off, a tall man with a child on each hand, skipping and singing.

Turning the corner into Branston Road we were in full voice ‘He really is a wizz of a wi ...’

Mummy was at the gate with Granny on the steps behind her.

‘Singing in the street! Whatever are you thinking? And where is the pram?’

‘It's Somewhere ... Over the Rainbow.’ Daddy sang. I could have sworn Granny sniggered. She bolted into the house followed by Mummy who slammed the door. We went round the back where Granny let us in.

Lunch was full of chatter, while Mummy spoke not a word. She fumed quietly for several days, but the awful pram was gone forever.

### *Biff! Thud!*

In the interests of fun, we were given popguns, miniature rifles that fired a cork attached by a short string. They lasted until we were caught kitten-hunting behind the shed

The little black cat my mother swapped for the pet mice was called Bijou, and was meant to be a 'wife' for Patchy who was black and white. She produced three kittens in the comfort of an old sheepskin flying-boot Daddy left unzipped on the floor. They were all ginger. Mummy seized Patchy and examined him closely swearing that he had been 'got at' by a vet.

We called the kittens Winken, Blinken and Nod, but after the hunting episode they went to other homes. The popguns were confiscated, and we were back to two cats and a tortoise. I said maybe Bijou had chosen to marry the ginger cat down the road, like the bride who ran off with Jock of Hazeldene.

'After all, you don't have to marry someone your family wants.' My parents looked at each other, and then at me. I couldn't read them at all.

The next innovation was the Saturday Morning Cinema, where dozens of unattended children watched ancient films with jittery streaks and crackling sound. Usually there was a cartoon, (Popeye, or Mickey Mouse), a children's News Reel, a space hero (Flash Gordon), a detective (Dick Tracy) and some knockabout comedy that I didn't like at all. (Laurel and Hardy, Abbott and Costello, Chaplin).

I didn't want to see people being unkind and thinking it was funny. I especially hated The Three Stooges, kicking and tripping, ripping clothes, and jabbing each other in the eyes. I blocked my ears and turned away when they were on. It's a genre I still find repellant.

But we all enjoyed the Westerns, Gene Autry, Roy Rogers, Hop-along Cassidy. We cheered madly for the Sheriff's posse (Hurray!) as it pursued the villains (Boooooo!) or Indians, though I was never quite sure about booing Indians. I suspected they had a lot in common with black people. I meant to ask Daddy, but forgot.

You couldn't make friends at the Saturday Pictures. You had to stay in your seat and behave. Stern usherettes patrolled the aisles keeping us all in order and it was too dark to socialise.

My father collected us after the show. Since Westerns were often the last shown, this meant a horde of children blinking into the daylight, pointing fingers at each other and yelling "Phteeew! Zoing!".

Falling down dead in the street when hit was not the done thing, (though fine in the schoolyard), so you just clutched your chest and staggered about a bit until you found your parent. I failed to notice that other little girls didn't do this.

### *What little girls are made of.*

My father bought six-shooter cap-pistols for us, to make up for the popguns and Granny added belts and appropriate hats. We ran riot in the garden for a while but they couldn't afford to keep us in caps and with no one to play with we lost interest. Mummy had other ideas anyway. I needed to be more lady-like.

I already knew there were rules about what you could wear, when and with whom, how to sit and stand, or place your feet. Mummy took me to a cafe called The Nook and taught me to tip my soup plate away from me and sip from the side of my spoon. There were special ways to use a napkin, or how to place your knife and fork. Life was a complicated dance, and I enjoyed the challenge.

Mummy's school was mornings only. In the afternoons she shopped and cooked. Twice a week, we had 'help', an invisible woman who used the back door and never came in further than the scullery, her presence betrayed only by the smell of bleach.

The rest of Mummy's time was spent at the theatre now that "Sunshine and Smiles" was back in town. On many days Granny was around when we got home from school, to give us our tea and cook for Daddy. She let us play outside with the Ibbots and other children that Mummy deemed beneath us.

I wasn't supposed to speak to Eunice Ibbot. All other children had lice, Mummy said. If we played with them we'd be sent home with a card from Nitty Norah, the school nurse. But Granny let us play, and it was Eunice that taught us "May I?" and "Queenie, Queenie" and "What's the Time, Mr Wolf?"

We played as long as we dared, listening for the whirr-clonk of Mummy's faulty bike chain; dashing indoors when we heard her coming. The other children understood but we did so want to make proper friends.

Mummy was telling people about the madness. We met another mother who asked if I could come to play, but Mummy said sadly, that I was not a well child and might have a funny turn.

I pleaded but she drew me to her side protectively and said gently, 'Now you wouldn't want to hurt anybody, would you?' The other woman looked at her in sympathy.

### *Runaway Rocking-horse.*

I'm not sure there would have been time for proper friends in Clacton, what with school, two dance classes in the week plus a triple class on Saturday afternoon, ballet, tap and acrobatics, and practice in between.

There was singing too, which Mummy taught me. Blowing silently at a candle flame. Seeing how long I could hold middle C. Starting notes soft and getting louder and then fading them away to nothing. I've never had my voice trained but this is obviously where I learned the control. I could be a star, Mummy said, if I worked hard.

We practised mime as well; how to move like people of different ages, and how to show your feelings with your back turned, by posture alone. It worked both ways though. I learned how *not* to show anything at all, so she couldn't see what I was thinking.

I'd always loved the dancing, partly as an escape from the pram, but mostly because I could stretch and reach and tumble and make special shapes with my body. Next year I could start taking exams.

I was nearly seven now, and old enough to walk alone to my classes. They were half a mile away and I had time to dance through the empty streets making up steps to tunes I liked. Currently it was "Runaway Rocking-horse", a complicated piece but as ever I could hear it in my head as I danced along.

I tried to start the movements as a toy, get more horse-like and slowly become a toy again. One afternoon, rounding the corner by the Westcliffe Theatre, two of the company were standing out front.

'What's all this?' cried one, flapping a hand. 'Do show!'

It was Chuck and Billy, a comedy duo. Babs, who was head of chorus, said they'd made films in Hollywood before the war. They whisked me into the empty foyer and helped me with my steps before sending me on my way. I did not know then how important they would become in my life.

Miss Thorogood was pondering a theme for the carnival concert. I showed her my rocking-horse dance and she built a magic toyshop sequence round it for the other children with dolls, bears, bricks and a tea set. Mummy added a mane and tail to my white vest and knickers and the rest of me was painted with whiting, as tights were unobtainable.

It was only a small hall but it didn't matter. I did my usual "Over the Rainbow" finale, Granny sat in the front row grinning from ear to ear, and I felt like a million dollars.

### *Lost and found.*

Mummy bought another pram, a dolls' pram this time, and Susan, my best doll, was installed therein.

'That'll slow you down,' my mother said, as we headed for the seafront, me trotting beside her with my pram. 'We need a little more decorum.'

Down at the beach hut, I sat on the terrace, writing in my notebook, occasionally tending my doll but wishing I could go onto the sand. Daddy and Daniel were off watching cricket. Granny was doing B&B now, so rarely came down in the day.

'You could take Susan for a walk.' Mummy said.

I put my notebook away and wheeled the pram off the terrace.

'Feet straight! Head up!' she called after me as I set off sedately down the prom.

I stopped as soon as I was out of sight. There was a beach up here where the tide came right up to the wall, and when it was out a man came and drew huge pictures on the damp sand and people threw him pennies. I sat on the steps and watched him for a while. What did I want? I loved my doll, and the pram was very smart, but really I just wanted to read books and write poems, and sing and dance and ... and ...

I remembered that when we lived in Birmingham Mummy used to leave me in odd places in my pushchair. Someone always brought me home. I walked the pram right down to Butlin's funfair and parked it up. I wrote a note with my name and address, and unhitched my satchel. I couldn't bear to leave Susan, so I used my bolero to sling her on my back like the African ladies in National Geographic Magazine and walked back to the hut.

'Where's the pram?'

'I don't know.' which was true. I knew where I'd left it, but it wouldn't be there now. I refused to say more. I was threatened with spanking but I was too fed up to care.

The pram was returned that evening, and when I'd used the same trick a couple more times the pram was sold and I got to run and skip and look in shop-windows again. The red swimsuit reappeared, along with Granny sometimes, and I got to turn cartwheels on the green sward beside the pier, or across the sand when the tide was out. That was better!

### *Miracles and magic.*

My Granny Soal's life revolved around her home at Skeena, and the Pier Avenue Baptist Church. We accompanied her there on Sunday mornings. I hated it. Stepping out over the threshold felt like returning to a world where everyone was doomed if they weren't a Baptist. It couldn't be right. God was supposed to love us all, and the King was Church of England wasn't he? Granny agreed but said she had to go because Grandad had been a minister. Mummy meanwhile spouted fire and brimstone, at least until we got home when she turned back into Bette Davis.

I had long realised that people had different views of God. I asked Daddy why he didn't come, and he said since God was everywhere you didn't have to go to church to find Him, or just one day of the week. You could talk to Him any time, but it was important for me to go as a kindness to Granny, and the more I learned the better I'd make up my mind when I was bigger. Fair enough.

Granny's view could be called 'practical Christianity' and was always comforting. She had a good fund of bible stories, could invent a prayer for any occasion, and called in angels to help with spells. For a child with a fever, a hand on your head and the other on your heart she'd say:

*'There came three angels out of the East.*
*One brought fire and one brought frost.*
*Out fire! In frost!'*

It always seemed to help, along with the Owbridge's Lung Tonic and Vick's Vapour Rub.

Granny said there was no difference between a spell and a prayer and magic was something God gave us to help things along. She and Mummy could both read tealeaves and dreams and palms and cards, and did charms against warts.

### *Roots and branches*

Thus it was that Mummy became a gypsy for the 1949 carnival, and did a roaring trade in a little tent near the pier. By the end of the week she was a *real* gypsy, instantly recognisable by anyone of Romany stock, many of whom had approached her in awe, she said, convinced she was somehow related. Her notes claim the Roma concerned were Younkman's Czardas Band, a gypsy orchestra. 'They only have to look at me,' she said, 'and they know.'

Mummy's claim to Romany blood came, she said, through Granny, to whom it was a matter of great shame. Just in herself had the negative qualities been filtered out leaving only her looks, her charisma, and her psychic powers.

Over the years my mother's imagined roots spread far and wide until, with the exception of orientals, Amerindians and blacks, she had a pick-n-mix wardrobe of world-wide DNA, which she wore like changing skins. In later years she sent my daughter lists of supposed blood relations, which included Royals, politicians, Hollywood Stars and a selection of British luvvies. The persona of Madame Zara, meanwhile, remained and proved lucrative for the rest of her life.

As for Younkman's Czardas Band, Nat Younkman was a Latvian Jew who came to Britain in the 1920s and settled in Manchester. His wife, Millicent was English, stage name Madame Ludmilla, and their daughters Pam and Dottie were also in the band. Other players came and went over the years, as they tend to do. The band specialised in Holiday Camps, especially after WW2, and was indeed in Clacton in 1949.

Younkman's was the only band in Britain playing that brand of music, mostly accordions and balalaikas plus a pianist. Whether Nat had Romany roots I do not know, but he and Millie are buried in the Jewish Cemetery in Manchester. So the internet tells me.

# Thirteen

Our Birmingham house had been late Art Deco, and almost new, its rear windows wrapped around corners in curving glass and furnished in similar style. The Clacton house was Edwardian but my mother faithfully reproduced the glamourous bedroom, occupying it now in solitary splendour, a holy space to which I was admitted rarely.

The blue bedspread was quilted in tiny fans, a family of blue china rabbits sat atop a tall-boy. A great circular mirror backed the waterfall dressing-table which held a mock tortoiseshell dressing set, a blue and white drum of rouge labeled Bourjois, a blue bottle of Evening in Paris scent, and a pot of pink gel for strengthening nails.

The floor was a work of art. The boards around the edge were stained black and polished, framing a pale blue carpet-square with no regular pattern or border. Like a painting by Miro, it bore a black squiggle here, a trio of short white lines there, an orange semi-circle in a corner. It was thick and soft.

In this glamorous boudoir my mother and I prepared for carnivals and concerts and amateur dramatics, in the three Clacton years. She seemed happy at those times. We were girls together, with powder and paint, and I wonder what fun we could have had later if only ... but I don't do 'if only'. It clutters up your life.

### Absence

After carnival, the holiday improved. We were at the beach-hut most days. Granny was less busy. Daddy was around. Mummy was preoccupied with her friends at the Westcliffe Theatre and was rarely seen before tea.

The beach was busy. The sea was warm. Daddy tried to teach us swimming. He put our arms through old cycle inner-tubes twisted into figures of eight and tied with tape.

We entered a castle contest. We watched Punch and Judy. And we went up to Butlin's to watch the doughnuts go round and round in their little pans, and ate them hot and sugary.

We ran on the beach alone too, and I took Daniel to see the man who drew in the sand. Sometimes a maroon went up, and we rushed down to see the boathouse open, and the lifeboat speed down the slipway and out to sea. And we put pennies in the big red mine that served as a moneybox for the RNLI.

There were more ships now. The minesweepers still patrolled the horizon, but when the tide was in, steamers came down the Thames, and docked at the end of the pier. The Royal Sovereign, cream and green; the Golden Eagle, black and gold, a paddle steamer that could turn on the spot by making the paddles go opposite ways.

Day-trippers, flooded off the pier, singing and larking about, paddling and squealing in the sea, like children. The sands were crowded by mid-day and as the tide came in everyone backed up the beach until they were huddled side by side.

I read the tide-tables posted by the pier. I watched for the turn, standing by the water's edge until the first little waves failed to make it up the wet bit. No one knew what I was doing. It was a secret between me and the sea. I concentrated. Mummy claimed I was having 'absences' but Granny had guessed and told her not to be silly.

Before school started we had a visit from more of the jolly relations we had seen in Lewisham during the war, sharing a cellar away from bombs. These were Granny's relations; her sister Lily and husband Frank Wadey.

Mummy was scandalised by the unseemly hugging as usual, and the fact that the ladies didn't always wear their corsets. Uncle Frank didn't care. Not so many years ago he had been dragged naked from the water at Dunkirk, and survived infected shrapnel, and severe shock. Every person and every moment was precious to him. To hell with corsets.

On some days Mummy arrived with food and we stayed to eat our tea. The crowd thinned and the air cooled. The shadows of the empty deck-chairs stretched out towards the pier. Then Daniel and I folded chairs for the deck-chair man, as we had last year, and rode on the trolley down the prom.

There was a feeling of things slowing down, becoming calmer. It's hard to name my favourite time of year, but end-of-summer could be it.

### *Medicine*

It was autumn. Time to be prim and proper and decently dressed for the walk to the school bus in Jackson Road. Daniel and I went on our own now, and were trusted to cross the roads. Not that there were many cars about. We didn't know anyone who had one except Grandad Innes in Birmingham.

I wished I could see Grandad. I wondered how he was ... and Grannie ... and the Uncles ... and cousin Pat who was mad like me and had fits. I didn't have fits yet, but Mummy said I had absences. It was only when I was thinking, or writing a poem in my head, or keeping still to watch insects or birds. Granny Soal knew, but Mummy insisted.

Sometimes I got angry and cried and protested, but tantrums were another sign of the madness, so I tried to keep very calm and still, but that was a sign of 'absence'. I couldn't win. Sometimes I was very afraid.

We went to the doctor. Mummy was concerned. She described the absences and the tantrums and cousin Pat's epilepsy. Dr Davey looked at me kindly. I burst into tears and protested.

'I don't have absences,' I said, 'Honestly.'

He leaned down towards me, and smiled. 'The trouble is,' he said, 'you wouldn't know.'

I panicked. I knew perfectly well, but I was trapped. I shook and cried, and Dr Davey got his dispenser to give us a bottle of bright blue medicine, which would calm me down. I didn't mind if it would stop me feeling so scared.

The blue medicine stood on the high kitchen mantelpiece when my father came home. I thought it looked rather pretty. Mummy went into full dramatic flow.

'THIS is for YOUR daughter. YOU are the cause. HOW could they let you marry?'

* * *

Daddy took the blue medicine and poured it down the sink. Then he phoned the surgery. Mummy put on her coat and went to the theatre.

I was called out of class a few days later to see the head. I wondered what I'd done. Dr Davey was there. I tried to say, politely, that I didn't have absences, but it only came out as a whisper.

'It's all right,' he said 'Your Daddy's explained, but we wondered if the problem is with your hearing, Mary, since you seem so far away. Miss Ault tells me you don't answer when you are called.'

I had never got used to being called Mary. I told them. 'I was Elizabeth Innes until we came to live here, but Mummy changed it and now I'm in Mr Jones class he can't say my surname either, so I don't know who Mary Inns is. I didn't mean to be rude.'

Miss Ault said we couldn't change the Mary but she would speak to Mr Jones about the Innes bit. He never did learn to say 'Innes' but called me Guinness, which was near enough for me to know when I heard it.

### *So many children ...*

The Old Woman Who Lived in a Shoe may not have known what to do with children, but my mother did. Her little school reassembled for the autumn term, and while the weather was still warm she took them for walks. They were impeccably behaved, and she liked to be seen about town with them, walking two-by-two holding knots on a long white rope.

She was often at the theatre when we got home so we went there sometimes after school. One afternoon, she was in the front stalls, hanging out with Chuck and Billy who were rehearsing a spoof on "Spectre de la Rose"... Chuck in a threadbare dressing-gown over his tights.

'I TOLD him!' Mummy said, 'the child needs MEDICINE! But he will NOT listen.'

'Oooh! ... Nice big slices of juicy HAM for supper!' said Chuck.

'I was NOT ham-acting!' said Mummy, 'I was in a PASSION!'

'Suit yerself!' said Chuck, flapping a hand.

So passion was allowed and wasn't the same as a tantrum. I pondered on what the difference might be. Tantrums seemed to be spur of the moment things, often called 'flying off the handle' but passion was thought out beforehand, at least Mummy's opening lines were, or the dramatic exits.

I imagined you used passion to let people know something was *very* important. I tried it in later years. It didn't work. After the first few words my passion took on a life of its own and got me into scrapes.

'It doesn't make sense, Win.' Granny said when Mummy held forth about the medicine. 'One minute she's a genius, then she's Shirley Temple, and now you want to be the mother of a sick child. You are not playing parts in a film!'

'What do YOU know?' Mummy said 'Brought up in the gutter!'

She often said that. God said to honour your father and mother, so why was she speaking to Granny that way? It can't be true, I thought, Granny has net curtains and proper shoes. Anyway, Granny refused to agree that I was mad, and Mummy would have to get around it herself, and Mummy said, mark her words, she would.

After that, madness was forgotten for a while because life got busy. "Sunshine & Smiles" was packing up but Mummy wasn't so upset this year as she knew they'd be back in the spring. Meanwhile there were new amateur productions to organise and rehearse, a concert in aid of the church, and my parents were both in a play for CADS. There would be costumes and make-up, and people in and out of the house at night, reading through their lines downstairs as I fell asleep. The grown-ups would be happy, and so would I.

### *Playing your part.*

Daddy had new pictures taken for front of theatre. He tried to look seriously thespian, but failed. He was 41, and despite being superbly fit and athletic, his hair was prematurely thinning and grey. What was left of it was slicked down with Brylcream, as was the fashion. He looked mischievous ... and well he might. He was planning something outrageous for the church concert.

Church concerts were always fun. People turned up and did a turn, not always well, but that wasn't the point. There was a clumsy conjuror, an uncoordinated acrobat and piano duettists who styled themselves Rabbits and Lawnmower (after Rawitz and Landauer). The audience applauded wildly and gave them full marks for trying.

I was to do "Over The Rainbow" again (while the dress still fitted), Granny was singing "The Keys Of Canterbury" with one of the deacons, and Mummy was doing "Three A'pence A Foot", a monologue about Noah.

Daddy was doing Shakespeare, Mark Anthony's speech from Julius Caesar. He rehearsed three steps up the stairs with his dressing gown draped over his arms like a body. Mummy made him a toga. She and her Roman ladies were to kneel on the stage gazing up at him in awe. They would be especially glamorous, with long tunics, and ribbons woven into their hair. 'Friends, Romans, countrymen ...' declaimed Daddy from the staircase, at every opportunity, 'I come to bury Caesar, not to praise him.' We reckoned he would be magnificent.

On the night, hidden by curtains, Daddy stood on a dais at the back of the stage, as Mummy and her Romans assembled in expectation. The curtains parted revealing Daddy, all six foot three of him, in a toga and sandals. He took a deep breath and, in his best Bogart/Cagney voice said ...

'Shay lishen you guys! Ged a load a dis! I've come to plant this guy Caesar, not to spill no publicity guff.'

I couldn't see Mummy's face, or hear most of the rest, as everyone was laughing so much. Finally Daddy paused for the laughter to subside and said, 'Brutus has told ya dat Caesar wiz on de up an up, an if dats on da level he sure got what was comin' to him.'

There was a standing ovation. Granny took off her glasses to wipe her eyes. Only Mummy said it wasn't funny.

I try when writing to stick to the observations and feelings of the time, in this case those of a seven-year-old. But, writing this, my older self feels suddenly sad for my mother. She could not connect with laughter or warmth and spontaneity. Everything had to be scripted and choreographed in accordance with a set of impossible standards that she felt duty-bound to uphold, and a picture of the world that was skewed beyond hope of repair.

We all have different things that tickle our funny-bones and it wasn't that Mummy never laughed. She found Joyce Grenfell funny, and Gracie Fields. She loved farce, and scripted comedy sketches where someone gets the better of someone else, or a servant exposes an embarrassing situation in a 'respectable' household. She was a gifted character actress with a whole range of voices and postures. It's just that for her it was a very serious business.

To the wider world Mummy was bright and vivacious and full of fun. She was the life and soul of any event, an endless procession of comic characters, and a gift to Clacton Amateur Dramatic Society.

She was thirty-two and knew she was too old for female leads and not old enough for the 'grande dame', so she opted for char-ladies, dizzy cousins, and awkward unmarried daughters. She rehearsed alone in her room, often in costume, and some nights when she tucked us in, we weren't sure who she was.

Voices were important. Home entertainment was mostly radio, and everything was conveyed by sound. At weekends we listened to 'ITMA', and 'Much-Binding-in-the-Marsh.' Kenneth Horne's voice was a bit like Daddy's. We listened to 'Dick Barton, Special Agent' and 'Paul Temple', and for us, 'Toytown', and 'Just William'.

### *Bad mad Daddy.*

I knew our family was unusual, and I wished we could be like The Famous Five who were always loved and forgiven, no matter what they did. In our house, every slip was added to my mass of past sins. I was getting badder and badder and one day God would do something about it and I would be finished. I tried not to think about that.

My father's disposal of the blue medicine was another sign of the madness. Mummy was upset. She got some more madness medicine. This time it was pills. I only had to take a quarter tablet when I was upset. Mummy crushed it between two teaspoons, adding a dab of jam. It was a bit gritty, and I didn't think I felt any better, but then I hadn't felt bad when I took it. Maybe I had to get more upset first.

Daddy was more of a problem. He had to have tablets every day but Mummy knew he wouldn't take them. They would have to go in his dinner. Mummy needed my help, she said, and a promise of secrecy. Daddy and I would be nicer and not have tantrums. We would all be happier. I promised. She put the pills between two sheets of baking paper and I rolled the Worcester Sauce bottle over them until they were powder.

I would have done anything to be in her good books so the madness medicine became our secret. I took mine with no trouble and the bottle lived behind the cutlery tray in the kitchen drawer. Nobody knew it was there but Mummy and me.

### *Deus ex machina*

I made a special writing for my notebook so that nobody could read it, although Daddy still wrote some of my other diary if there was a lot to tell. He kept it in his room in the padlocked metal deed-box that had been to Jamaica. The room smelled of pipe-smoke and feet so I never stayed long, and of course I never said a word about the medicine.

Mummy was worried about some of her pupils. She thought she had spotted signs of the 'epileptic disposition' in some of them, and even more worrying things in others. Beside her plate at teatime she had a pile of foolscap sheets, each with a pair of little handprints. She peered at them with a spyglass, reading their palms. One, she said, would become a killer, and another his victim.

Daddy got irritable and said it was poppycock. Mummy said it was her duty to find evil. It was the job God had set her. Grandad Soal and Mummy were chosen by God, she said, at the beginning of time, to be saved and go to heaven with the elect. Evil on earth had to be measured so that God knew who to bring low in life.

Mummy used a special voice when she talked like this. It cut the air and I longed for her to stop.

‘You're not telling their parents this rubbish I hope.’ said Daddy.

‘Of course not! They too are tainted. I just need to keep an eye in them discreetly.’

‘Oh I see! God's secret agent! UTTER BAL ... DERDASH!" Daddy left the room slamming the door. Daniel started to cry. I hated it when Daddy shouted. It was so very loud.

I wanted to know how God and heaven fitted in with the sun and the planets and atoms. Daddy took us to see “Fantasia” and though it didn't answer my question, the 'big bang' idea made more sense than heaven and hell, but I was still confused. I just wished grown-ups would make up their minds.

### *Season of mists*

As winter approached the sea grew greyer and the waves higher. In bed at night we could hear the foghorn mooing like a lost cow. It was the new school year and Daddy called it ‘Season of lists and callow youthfulness.’ which had something to do with the new boys in his class.

Breakfast changed back from cornflakes to porridge. There was toast and dripping, tea, woolly gloves and school coat, and a steamy-breath wait at Jackson Road for the bus to Holland Park School. The delicious contrast between my warm insides and the cold outside is one of my favourite feelings still. Sometimes Daddy took the bus instead of the train and waited with us, doing pull-ups on the bottom rung of an iron ladder high on the wall, to impress our friends.

When Mummy was out we still played in the street sometimes. I was protective of Daniel. I couldn't do it at school as he was in another playground, but in our street I threatened to biff anyone who teased him for his stammer, like Mummy did.

We heard that the other children had a den up at the coach-park. We found Carol there, in the bushes, asking a penny a time for a peek at her little brother's winkle. Well, honestly! I'd already seen one. I had a little brother too. I took Daniel home before she could include him in the merchandise. Male anatomy was no mystery to me, so I wasn't about to pay Carol to look at it.

With hot water and soap in short supply, Daniel and I had always bathed together. The differences in our bodies were simply God's design features, to show the difference between boys and girls. Boys' extra bits were delicate and a bit of a liability I thought. I was glad I was a girl.

The vulnerability of the extra bits was becoming an issue now, as our legs grew longer and it was hard not to kick each other in the groin. We had to bathe one after the other which wasn't fun at all.

Bathing at Skeena had always been best; the whumph! of the copper geyser as it lit; the steamy room. Standing up afterwards, (careful not to hit your head on the geyser spout) and waiting to be wrapped in big warm towels; and Granny's arms steadying us as we stepped out of the bath. She had a big chest that was soft as you bumped against it. This was a design feature of grown up ladies and was called a bosom. Men didn't have bosoms. They had bristles.

We spent Christmas at Skeena, along with the very old aunts. The cake was a Viking long-ship with iced shields. Our sled became another long-ship. Daniel wore a tunic and cross-garters and I wore my nightie with a golden girdle and long yellow plaits of knitting-wool. We towed it into the sitting room loaded with small family gifts on Boxing Day.

Our bigger presents were the usual Hornby rolling stock, and for me, several dolls, in an attempt to wean me off space-rockets and Meccano, but though Mummy gave me all her old "Josephine and her Dolls" books, it didn't work.

The Aunts were as lovely as ever. Auntie Mary was eighty and showed us the birthday letter she had from Queen Mary, who remembered her coming to Marlborough House and Sandringham "to nurse his late majesty and other family members."

George V was a naval man, and Auntie Mary always said 'We knew His Majesty was getting better when the volume and variety of his oaths returned to normal.'

How a greengrocer's daughter from Lewisham came to be nursing the King of England, is a whole other story. But Auntie Mary had trained at the Greenwich Seamen's Hospital and the language would have bothered her not a jot.

# *Fourteen*

The first innovation of 1950 was tricycles. I wanted one with a boot which was too expensive, but I did have a basket on the front, proudly carrying my tap and ballet shoes to class. Sometimes, muffled up in gloves and scarves, Daniel and I pedaled off to Granny's on our own for tea. We seemed to spend a lot of time there.

My mother was proud of her little school, and when we had colds we stayed at Granny's so as not to pass it on. Granny tucked us up in the big spare bed, with hot-water bottles and Vicks rub, or wrapped us in rugs by the fire listening to the wireless. For sore throats we had hot milk with honey and a knob of melted butter to soothe as it went down.

The interrogation came afterwards. There were only two ways children became ill, Mummy said; kissing ... and guilt. So who had we kissed? What had we stolen?

'Nobody, Mummy, nothing, honestly.' It would be all right when we were grown-ups. Adults got ill when they were 'sorely tried', usually by children. This was called 'A cross to the bear.' Like Jesus.

There was an election. What was a vote? Grown-ups had to put a secret cross on a paper to say who would be Prime Minister. When it was all over Mr Atlee was still in charge. Mummy was disgusted and said it wasn't worth voting.

Daddy pointed out that Auntie Mary's sister Ruth had been a suffragette. 'She nearly got arrested.' Daddy said.

'Served her right,' said Mummy, 'Making an exhibition of herself.'

'It's people like Ruth that got you the vote.'

'And a lot of good it's done me,' Mummy said, 'Grubby little socialists.'

Daddy said we must be thankful for the Health Service and make good use of it. Mummy said she intended to, and consoled herself by getting yet another cat, tortoiseshell and white, full-grown and possibly a stray. We called her Tabitha Twitchet after the Beatrix Potter character. She disappeared within weeks.

We searched the streets on our tricycles, calling her name, accompanied by Daddy on his bike, but Mummy reckoned she'd been stolen and was probably a pair of gloves by now.

Daddy read us "The Cat Who Walked By Himself" and he thought Tabitha was 'out in the wild wet woods, waving her wild tail and walking her wild lone' as Rudyard Kipling said.

### *Glorious isolation*

My tendency to think for myself worried my mother. Acting independently was all part of the madness, as were any kind of tears or protests. I tried to control it, and took my 'madness medicine' like a good girl when I failed. Daniel didn't have the madness but was tainted in some other mysterious way. We were Satan's children and it was Mummy's job to save the world from the terrible things we might do.

Granny said it was nonsense. We didn't know what to think. Other adults sometimes addressed us as 'little devils' so we thought it must be true. I felt sorry for Mummy having to look after us. She seemed so beautiful and clever, and knew everything. Why had God given her such bad children?

Although Daniel and I shared the big bed at Granny's, ever since my attempt to walk to France along the beach, we were kept apart at home. Our playroom was now the nursery school, so we played alone in our rooms.

It proved to be just as well when in mid-April, with term hardly started I woke up one morning with tiny red spots all over my chest and arms. I had scarlet fever. Mummy actually screamed.

'Back to bed! NOW! Don't be frightened! Mummy knows what to do!'

Naturally I was scared stiff. Mummy put up a notice saying the school was closed. I watched from my window as baffled parents turned away. Dr Davey confirmed the diagnosis, issued medicine and instructions, and a man came round and put a big red sticker on our door.

## SCARLET FEVER

**Keep out of this house**

**By order of the Board of Health**

I was ill for a long time. Two other children at school got it and were hospitalised, but Daniel didn't get it so playing separately proved a good thing that time. He went to stay with Granny. Daddy stayed with a friend in Colchester and Mummy and I settled in for the duration. Six weeks in total.

Scarlet fever is still a notifiable disease, although the strain has weakened over the years. In 1950 it was a killer. There could be many complications; rheumatic fever, kidney failure, toxic shock. It could weaken your heart. You *had* to be quarantined.

I slept for most of the first week. The headache was dreadful, my throat was raw, and I often felt queasy. I remember being woken in the night to take medicine. Mummy and the doctor wore masks and gowns, which were put in a bucket of disinfectant on the landing and boiled every day.

My plates and cutlery were washed in the room and dunked in boiling water and Dettol. Towels, face-flannels and sheets went straight into disinfectant and were boiled in the gas-copper.

My room was the little one over the front door, with just room for a bed, and a little desk and chair. There were no books or toys, which was just as well because the fumigation team would burn them when I was better. I *was* going to get better ... though I knew not everyone did.

Seven-year-olds did not know about sex in 1950, but we knew about death. We talked about it in the playground. We all knew someone who had lost a sibling or classmate to something. Sometimes it was one of us. Diphtheria. Polio. Meningitis. We didn't hug as children do now. We patted shoulders and called each other 'old man' and 'old thing' as our fathers did. You didn't have to fight a war to die young.

So I knew I might die, but I wasn't afraid. There was no point. I was more afraid of the inquest into how I'd caught it, though at the moment Mummy was being an absolute star.

In the second week my temperature went down but I ached all over and was very weak. Mummy was in her element. She switched roles seamlessly from teacher to nurse, waiting on me with egg custards, junkets and jellies and, once I could swallow properly, macaroni cheese and fish pies. Granny took charge of the ration books and shopped for us daily, leaving the bags on the step.

I was alone most of the time, but I didn't mind. Although there were no books I had the daily paper and piles of comics. There was a new one, the Eagle, which we'd ordered for Daniel, but since he was at Granny's I had it instead, and discovered Dan Dare and Captain Pugwash.

Dr Davey said I would be infectious until my skin peeled off. We waited. It didn't happen. I was disappointed. I had expected to see my muscles laid bare like the pictures in Daddy's books. Eventually at the end of May, I was declared clear. I had been in bed six weeks.

### *Up and about*

I was weak and wobbly. The house seemed big and smelled of polish and coal. I had grown, and my shoes were tight. My hair had grown too. Granny was afraid they might shave my head but Mummy washed my hair in camphor solution before I left my room and the doctor said that was enough. It was funny lying with my head over the edge of the bed being shampooed, then standing in the basin to be washed down and stepping onto the landing with no clothes on, all fresh and new and free of germs.

The fumigators came and steamed my room with something smelly. My mattress was steamed, but the blankets and eiderdown were incinerated along with all the comics. The door was sealed with tape for a while before we were let back in. Then Mummy painted the room and it was mine again.

Daniel came home at last and we were both dosed up with malt extract, Bovril and vitamins. There were puddings, and custard, in bowls that didn't taste faintly of Dettol. Daddy came home too. My legs were like sticks. He said I needed to use my muscles so my tummy knew where to send the food. Otherwise it would just be fat. We took my tricycle out and I puffed along the pavement while he walked beside me. I managed as far as the corner in a week and all the way to Granny's in a month.

There was no inquest into how I caught the germs, even though Mummy had closed her school forever. She'd missed the return of Sunshine & Smiles too, back for a third season at the Westcliffe. Rather than get angry, she had formulated a new plan for my future. She would make me a star. I would sing, and dance, and act. And Mummy would see it went well. We sat on the edge of my bed.

'It wasn't so bad, was it, having to stay in a little room by yourself?' She was using her kind voice.

'No.' I said, truthfully.

I had thought it peaceful. There was no talk of madness, and no going on and on at meals while we watched Daddy trying not to answer, until he just got up and left the room.

'No,' I said, 'It was all right.'

Mummy said I would need to be brave. Like cousin Pat I would start to have fits soon. I would live in hospital, in a room on my own so that I didn't hurt anyone.

(*Oh I didn't want to hurt anyone ... EVER!*)

But if I was a good girl, and learned my dancing and singing, I could be famous and Mummy would collect me for rehearsals and shows and make sure I got back safely. I could learn to act. Shirley Temple was going to retire, Mummy said. I could be famous. It didn't sound so bad.

Then Mummy said, 'Of course you won't be able to get married or have babies, darling. Epileptics aren't allowed.'

I cried then, and she cuddled me, which was a rare treat.

### *Rocket men.*

I was soon back at school, with my hair in plaits which I'd always wanted. People stayed away from me in case I was still 'poisonous', but mostly because I smelled like a mothball. Camphor was my mother's new friend. Mixed with gum-Arabic and water it lived in a jam jar labelled 'STICKUM' and according to Mummy, was what Queen Nefertiti used in Egypt, to keep her hair tidy. It was combed through my hair before braiding, and woe betide me if one wisp escaped before I came home. It showed I'd been 'playing' so along with not wanting to crease my frock, I felt safer sitting in the bike shelter watching everyone else.

I became a people-watcher and made notes in my secret writing. Girls did circle-games, or skipped. (I wouldn't have minded a skipping rope.) Daniel was in a different playground because he was bullied for his stammer, but the boys in mine spent most of their time galloping about with their caps back-to-front, slapping their sides and pretending to be jockeys; Gordon Richards usually.

Mummy's schoolroom at home was empty of pupils now, but she still read their palm-prints over meals, pronouncing on their fates and characters. One teatime she grabbed my hand and declared that I would die under a train. 'Like in "The Red Shoes." she said.

'What's "The Red Shoes"?'

Mummy said, 'Never you mind!'

Daddy jumped to his feet. His chair had a taller back than the rest, with lots of long spindles. He leaned over it, gripping the sides, as Mummy held forth about my future. He was gripping very hard. Suddenly, with a crack and a rattle, the spindles detached from the chair and fell like pile of pick-a-sticks. Mummy fell silent. Daddy looked down and said,

'I think I've got some glue somewhere.'

I laughed. So did Daniel. We couldn't stop. Mummy just sat there. I don't think she knew a reaction to fit.

Not surprisingly, Daniel was upset about his Eagle comics. It wasn't just that I had read them, but the fumigators had taken them to be burned. They were the very first issues and he would never see them. He threw a tantrum. I offered to fill him in on what had happened to Dan Dare so far, but he said girls shouldn't know about space-men and rockets, and I threw a tantrum of my own.

Suddenly we were quarrelsome and at odds. Daddy said girls could do anything. So could boys; sewing; nursing. This was not helpful. Daniel said he wasn't a pansy and burst into tears.

Daddy couldn't win. He took us to a film called "Destination Moon". He told us about light-years and weightlessness. The men had to scream as the rocket took off to balance the pressure in their ears. They walked about in magnetic boots that clanked on the walls. I decided to be an astronaut. Daniel said I should have been left at home.

We had been apart six weeks. He'd had Granny all to himself and didn't want to share her. We had both missed Daddy and didn't want to share him either. I understood somehow that Daniel was adopted when nobody cared about him, and he needed someone of his own to stand up for him, but I was his big sister. It ought to be *me*.

Something else had changed while I was ill, and although in the town of Clacton we were still the popular Innes family, involved in everything, at home I sensed something had broken that couldn't be mended.

***Tap-step-ball-change.***

It was back to the dancing. Joan Thorogood held the junior class in Mummy's school-room for a while, until our little metal toes tapped the pattern off the Lino and we went back to the hut by her house. I was weak and out of practice. My limbs were all over the place. I tried a cartwheel and my arms gave way.

I was upset, but as the weather warmed we opened up our hut and spent more time at the beach. Daddy drew rows of circles in the damp sand. We hopped and jumped between them. We slalomed around them with a ball. My accuracy improved. We had 'wheelbarrow' races to strengthen my arms. Daddy explained I was growing. My memory didn't keep up with the length of my arms and legs. All the boys he taught had the same problem. It wasn't my fault. Mummy said the same.

Daddy had put on weight before I was ill, but came home brighter, fresher and a bit thinner. Mummy said to be careful since there'd been no one to put the madness medicine in his dinner. I went back to crushing up the tablets as before.

We gave Daddy a wide berth most of the time, but Mummy went down to the theatre at night, and he was a different person. He sang to us as he always had. I asked him if the Innes family were really mad. 'Mad?' he said 'They are furious.' It was a corny joke even then.

'It's not funny, Daddy! Mummy says we get it from the dastardly Sir Robert who helped to murder the Bonny Earl of Moray.'

*'Ye Hielans and ye Lawlans'*, sang Daddy.
*'Oh whaur hae ye been?'*

There was a song! We learned it.

'Mummy says they were all thugs and murderers, and it's in our blood.'

Daddy reckoned we had learned to behave in the last 700 years. It was *that* long? Gosh! But I worried that he wasn't taking it seriously.

### *A trip up to town*

The Making Mummy Happy project was still active, from my father's point of view. It was "Sunshine & Smiles" last season at the Westcliffe and perhaps he hoped her obsession with them would fade once they left. Using their shared love of the theatre he planned a few days in London for her, and bought tickets for "Carousel".

We didn't go to Granny's while they were away. She came to us. I remember because I woke one morning in my own room to find that they were back, and across the foot of my bed was laid a pair of pink and white striped shorts with a bib and braces, and an assortment of new hair-ribbons in checks and stripes. Daniel had a new outfit too.

For a while my mother was truly bright and animated, happy, excited. She enjoyed "Carousel" but they had also seen a woman called Ruth Draper who did monologues, and was an influence on Joyce Grenfel. Character performance was Mummy's great talent, and the trip inspired her.

The effect lasted several weeks. Daddy, meanwhile, sang in his bath, Billy Bigelow's soliloquy about children and we sat on the stairs to listen:

*'My boy Bill ...'*
('That's you, Daniel.')

*'I don't give a damn what he does, as long as he does what he likes.'*
('Daddy said damn!' ... 'It's all right, Daniel. It's in the song.')

*'My little girl, pink and white as peaches and cream is she.'*

It meant a lot to my father, and the soliloquy became his regular bath-time song.

# *Fifteen*

Skeena wasn't a grand house. It was a bungalow, or pretended to be, it's upper floor hidden from the street. It was built by double-great Auntie Lizzie and her husband in the early 1930s and modeled on ones they had known in Canada.

The master bedroom was downstairs, but there were two more in the roof. In one, squeezed into an alcove, was a single bed where Granny slept. The rest of the room was filled almost wall to wall by a billiard table, said to have been lowered in by crane as the house was built. On wet days and winter days Daniel and I potted balls for hours, keeping score with the sliding scoreboard on the wall.

### *Tea with Auntie Mary.*

Sometimes we had tea with Auntie Mary next door, just Daniel and me on our own. She was another of the double-greats, born in Poplar in 1867 where her father sold fruit from a barrow. Inside her tiny sitting-room was another world: genteelly scruffy and redolent of lavender. There were black velvet cushions embroidered with golden peacocks, a square table, its green plush cover fringed with bobbles, and hanging above it, an etched glass lampshade of deep pink with a long brass chain to control the gas.

Auntie Mary, beside the fire, wore black as softly faded as the room; long skirts, little boots, and a short velvet jacket, fur-edged, and closed at the waist by a single huge button of elaborately knotted cord. Beside her, in a cabinet, was a collection of Coronation and Jubilee china such as many people had. When she died in 1956, her life had stretched across five reigns.

Yet this was no ordinary collection. Between the mugs and trinket-boxes were signed photographs in silver frames; a child with a toy boat "from Louis": two women in ermine signed "Beatrice" and, in another hand, "Victoria Eugenie", and on the wall, George V as a young man signed simply

"George". Auntie Mary nursed Queen Victoria at the end of her life. Though if you mentioned it, she just said 'That poor old lady.' and fell silent.

Auntie Mary had a way with children. They would do anything for her, and we were no exception. She taught us our manners, how to use napkins, how to cut our food, to look after other people at table, and how not to be sloppy. If we were clumsy, she likened us to Mr Rass Pateen, a bogeyman of monstrous visage and vile habits who spilt food on his shirt and beard and spoke only in a gurgling growl.

Auntie Mary was discreet about the death of Victoria, but told us she had nursed the King and his brothers through chicken-pox, and been on holiday abroad with a little boy who wasn't allowed to cut himself in case he bled to death.

We never doubted her word, but it was only in the 1990s that I saw the published recollections of Sir James Reid, the Royal Physician, and had documentary proof. His detailed account of the queen's death matched Auntie Mary's and even mentioned "Nurse Soal seated on the bed." Nowadays I know even more about this magical lady and wouldn't have guessed that Mr Rass Pateen was an infamous Mad Monk, far less that she had met him.

Mary and her sister Sarah were rebels. Sarah joined the Salvation Army when it was seen as subversive, like joining CND in the 60s. She married a fellow officer and was involved in providing food for dockers in the great strike of 1889, and met Karl Marx's daughter Tussie. Auntie Mary was there too, assisting the Princess Christian (Queen Victoria's daughter Helen) through whom she ended up nursing the Queen. Sarah and her husband went on to run the SA Mens Hostel at Tooting. There were six sisters in all and every one of them carved her own path. Auntie Lizzie's, CV is even more remarkable.

### *A big girl now.*

At the end of July Daddy and I went to Birmingham on our own. Daniel had been unsettled by my quarantine and opted for a stay at Skeena instead. I hadn't seen my Innes grandparents for three years, but now they were having a Golden Wedding. We were going to a party.

The journey was my late birthday treat. I hadn't been on a train since we moved, and I waited for the thrill of the big engine-wheels passing my face, but I was taller now, and they didn't seem so dangerous.

We had lunch on the train. There were real dining-chairs and silver cutlery. I wrote it all down afterwards. I had never felt so posh. There were waiters in short white jackets with a point at the back, and instead of soup, entree and desert, there were *five* courses.

We had a transparent soup called consommé with a bit of parsley floating on top and then fish, a lonely creature abandoned on a big white plate with tomato sauce draped across its middle. Then there was lamb with new potatoes and peas, a peach Melba, and finally, my first ever cup of coffee and a biscuit with a bit of cheese called Stilton which I didn't like as much as ordinary cheese. Then Daddy smoked his pipe.

Outside Snow Hill Station, Birmingham had changed. There was still a man drawing pictures on the pavement, but the other beggars had gone; the men with suitcases of wind-up toys; the blind accordionist. It seemed a bit dull. But the buses were still blue and cream, and the flower ladies sat on the steps of the arcade. It dawned on me that things change, people change, including me, and the changes would never stop.

Grannie and Grandad's house hadn't changed at all; the pretty tiled hall, the tall clock, the stairs with the swirly bannister, a marble table with a dinner gong and the door to the kitchen where someone we never saw did most of the cooking.

Grandad said it was a lovely surprise and picked up the phone.

'They're here!' ... 'Eric and Elizabeth.' ... (so lovely to be Elizabeth again.) ... "It's all right, we can make a bed up for her here.'

Very soon Uncle Harry and Uncle Gordon arrived with the Aunties in tow and there was a lot of hissy whispering.

Grandad took me into the garden. I hoped he would take me out in his little red car again.

'I was in a lot of hot water for that.' he said. He didn't have the MG any more. He had turned it over from going too fast.

'I was lying upside down with petrol running up my trouser legs,' he said, 'Grannie was cross.' I could imagine.

'Why is she here?' ... 'She shouldn't have come.' ... 'Why did you bring her?' Daddy was in trouble. He shouted at Uncle Gordon.

Hilda said 'She can't stay here. The beds will be damp.'

Daddy said the beds were fine, but in the end I went to Uncle Harry and Auntie Rosa and hardly saw Daddy for the rest of the trip. Not that I minded. Pat was home for the party and I could ask her what it was like to live in hospital and have fits.

### *A glimpse of my future*

Cousin Pat was a shock. She was sixteen now. I knew we would both be bigger, but though she still had her cloud of soft curls, the pretty Pat of my early years was gone. She was fat and clumsy with spots round her chin from the medicine she took. She still loved me though and talked to me about hospital. She said it wasn't too bad. We were kindred spirits, she said, and I hoped we'd be in the same hospital when my fits started.

Auntie Hilda forbade my plaits because their Janet had them and would be upset, so Auntie Rosa curled my hair up in rags overnight and said I looked a million dollars.

The party was a lunch at Grandad's cafe in the Soho Road. Most of Purus Bakeries staff was there. We had salad. There was veal and ham pie with egg in the middle, and tiny chicken tarts called 'vollervons' which Daddy said was French for a puff of wind.

Uncle Gordon was still grumbling. Granny said, 'It's not the child's fault.' and Grandad sat me next to him and gave me the crunchy bones from his tinned salmon. The press took pictures. There were speeches, but nobody sang anything.

Grannie and Grandad's house was a Victorian time-warp, Uncle Gordon's prim and pristine, but Uncle Harry's was battered and bruised where Pat's crashing falls had knocked hell out of the furniture. Despite Pat being hospitalised, she came home at weekends so it wasn't worth replacing things. The black wire fireguard and its brass rail were buckled and bent. There were no ornaments. Nevertheless it was warm and comfy, like Auntie Rosa.

Uncle Harry was a nervy man. He chain-smoked, his fingers brown with nicotine. He was 'Mr Harry' of Purus Bakeries. He worked hard, and was the one who rose at four every morning to start making bread. He took his daughter's affliction very badly.

After the anniversary lunch I went home with Auntie Rosa and Pat ... and Pat had a seizure. It must have been the excitement. She went down sideways with an almighty crash. I looked over the arm of the sofa and she was there on the floor thrashing. I'd seen it before when we were younger, but now she was almost a woman, and her bulk made it all the sadder. I knew she would stop in a minute, but it crossed my mind that I would look like that one day, and I hoped people would know what to do.

When Pat was still we covered her with a rug and put a cushion under her head. She had wet her nice frock and I felt embarrassed for her. The men were at Grandad's playing billiards, but Uncle Harry was summoned to help get Pat off the floor and I walked round to see Auntie Hilda who detailed Janet to take me to the park.

It was a grey afternoon. I thought we might get to know each other, but Janet was ten and I was quite beneath her notice. I followed her down the road, several paces behind promising myself I'd have plaits as long as hers one day. We sat side by side on the swings, but Janet didn't talk. We looked at the ducks. Then we walked back. Next morning Daddy and I were on the train home. He was very quiet so I just read my book.

Back in Clacton it was carnival time. Earlier in the year there was a fire at the Westcliffe Theatre, which Mummy had predicted. On the strength of that she was making good pin-money in her Madam Zara persona, with readings and secret séances.

She had recently branched out into spells, which she claimed to have learned through her ancestors in the Forest of Dean. She was, she said, the real McCoy, so for carnival 1950 she was a Witch. We moulded her prosthetics with theatrical 'nose putty' and steamed an old felt hat into a point.

Daddy reckoned Mummy was asking to get arrested but she said the Witchcraft Act was being overturned and then she could turn him into a toad with impunity. Daddy said Woolworths was fresh out of impunity and would have to order some more. We laughed, but there was an uncomfortable undercurrent as always.

I told Mummy about Pat and asked if I would look like that when I had fits. She said I should have my pills every day now, and not just when I got upset. Since it meant getting a teaspoonful of jam, I took them without complaint.

There was a film of Treasure Island about this time, and we went about rolling our eyes and calling people "matey". Robert Newton played Long John Silver and Mummy said he was a dirty old man because he had patted her bottom once when she was an extra in one of his films.

There were other good things in 1950 too. There was a new princess. We saw a newsreel of mountaineers and I wondered if girls could do that. Colchester United got into the Football League. Daddy was ecstatic. Now his boys had something to work towards. Even Daniel reckoned he would play for them when he grew up. He and Daddy got seriously into training, and sometimes they let me join in. I was still weak from the scarlet fever so it helped my legs get stronger.

### *Rehearsal*

My mother's voice could be penetrating, even when she spoke quietly. Shouting, she said, was a sign of mental derangement. Sometimes her voice got quite loud and Granny said, 'There's no need to raise your voice.'

Mummy said, 'I do *not* raise my voice. I PROJECT!'

Projecting was what actors did. My parents were both members of the Clacton Amateur Dramatic Society and as summer ended they were exploring possibilities. Mummy wanted CADs to put on a particular play so that she could audition for the lead. Daddy helped her run through. They rehearsed in the back parlour after we were in bed. Mummy liked the window open for fresh air. It could get very loud but we knew it was just a play. I had seen the words in the book.

One afternoon fetching in the washing, Mummy was talking to our neighbour.

'Did you hear him last night?' she said, 'I'm so scared of him.'

The neighbour sympathised. Mummy quoted some of the threats. The neighbour nodded. Mummy went indoors.

'It's only a play.' I said.

'I expect it is.' said the neighbour. She didn't believe me. I ran indoors for the book.

'Look! The words are here! Daddy was just reading them. It's called "Pink String and Sealing Wax". Daddy's a good actor too.'

The neighbour said, 'Oh dear'.

I didn't want to believe Mummy told lies. Only bad people did that and Mummy wasn't bad ... was she?

### *Open mouth. Insert foot.*

Summer ended. The new term started. "Sunshine and Smiles" left Clacton for the last time. Daddy was getting fat again, and sluggish and grumpy. He still sang and read stories at night, but we annoyed him a lot. He shouted. We cried. He stomped off to his room.

Mealtimes were the worst. Our parents sat at opposite ends of the table with Daniel and I between them. Mummy got more critical and dramatic. Daddy was ordered to phone the laundry, the milkman, the council, etc. to register her complaints. He closed his eyes and leaned his head against the wall. There was a greasy patch where his Brylcreem soaked into the paper. Sometimes Mummy leapt up grabbing the bread-knife, pressing her back to the wall, with the point beneath her breastbone.

'DO ... IT!'

I wondered if she should just go ahead, but she would bleed on the rug and spoil it. Then I felt guilty for wishing her harm. Meanwhile Daddy shuffled off to make the call while Mummy said

'See! What did I tell you? He's a dangerous man!' Adding, 'and YOU are his daughter.'

It didn't make sense.

Soap came off ration and Mummy bought Lux, as used by film stars, but only she could use it. The rest of us used Fairy Green. One night as Mummy scrubbed my back in the bath I said, without thinking. 'What do you call it when someone tells fibs to make someone else look bad, when they've not done anything wrong?'

'I have no idea what you mean.'

'Never mind, I'll ask Daddy.'

Mummy hurled the block of Fairy into the bath water and stalked out of the room. Oops!

So I did ask Daddy and he said that sort of fib was called a 'set up' and we explored the meaning of 'set', from jellies to dentures, from winter setting in, to people setting out, and I learned that a 'set up' could be anything from a harmless joke to a dangerous revenge. I didn't say anything about the play.

### *A deep breath*

I developed eczema. We went to the doctor. 'Asthmatical eczema runs in my family,' Mummy said, 'Mary has trouble breathing at night.' I said I didn't.

Dr Davey said I must be honest and not just brave, and gave us a note for a Rybar Inhaler and a bottle of stuff to put in it.

I had tummy-ache often too, and was sent home from school. I was not to eat meat, Mummy said. Doctor's orders. She would send a note to school. No note was sent.

I pleaded with dinner-ladies and teachers, but had to sit behind in the empty dining hall over cold stew. I stuck it out and became so distressed that the head phoned Dr Davey. I don't know what he said but apparently I could eat meat again and she thought Mummy had made a mistake. I wanted to say 'My foot!' But didn't dare. You didn't tell tales on grown-ups. It only made them worse.

The Rybar inhaler was used at night though I knew I didn't need it. It had a hard mask that hurt my face, and the inhalant smelled awful. It made my head swim and ache. I knew it was to help me sleep so I faked a couple of deep breaths, and let my head drop to one side. That's how you went unconscious in films. I'd seen it at the Saturday Cinema. It worked every time.

### *Fact and friction*

Daddy stopped coming to Sunday lunch at Granny's. Daniel and I ate our roast while Mummy held forth about her violent husband. Granny said 'Hrrumph!'

Mummy persisted. 'You'll see! They'll find me one day with my throat cut.' Granny harrumphed again. Daniel looked worried.

'You can't cast yourself in the lead of other people's dramas, Win. Life is not a film set.'

There were mutterings about 'Poor murdered Mabel'. I'd heard of her before, but no one would tell me more.

Breakfast at home got worse. The Making Mummy Happy project had slipped away. She needed to be around theatre people, but they were gone, and who knew what would be at the Westcliffe next summer.

Daddy was always tired now. Mummy wondered how he had the nerve to call himself a sports teacher. 'Bunny Baron would make *two* of you.' she said, 'and Robert Donat *three*!"

I just wanted Mummy to stop! Her voice bored into my head. I thought, 'Do something, Daddy! Make her stop!' and then I realised what he might have to do and she would die and he would be hanged, and I changed my thought to a prayer.

'Please, God, help Daddy not to lose his temper.'

He'd never hit anyone yet, but he was sitting with his fists clenched each side of his plate. I was really scared.

I took my acrobatics exams at last. I took Grades 1&2 on the same day and didn't do very well, 78 and 76 per cent. I'd lost confidence as well as coordination. The floor of the hall was rough and we spent the evening pulling splinters from my palms. I did so want to be like Eunice Ibbot's sister Doris who was sixteen and made like rubber, but eventually my body grew long and my legs stayed short. It was not to be.

There was still the occasional calm, chatty breakfast. I asked Mummy how long llamas lived. She thought it would be ten or twelve like cats and dogs, but then nothing lived very long in South America.

'But this one is fifteen and lives in Tibet. I heard it on the news.'

Mummy actually laughed. 'That's a Dalai Lama.'

Ah! So there were llamas in more than one country. I wondered if they had different size ears like elephants. Daddy said he would explain about Buddhism sometime. Mummy said he would do no such thing.

It was Mummy's birthday on the November 19th and Daddy bought her a book. It had a yellow cover and flew past my face before hitting Daddy in the chest. 'I just thought you'd enjoy some new flights of fancy.' he said.

Daddy retrieved the book and read us the stories for bedtime. "Tales of Baron Munchausen." No one had come up with the idea of a syndrome at that time, but maybe my father was onto something.

We enjoyed the stories anyway. How the Baron wounded a stag with cherry stones, and shot it years later with a full-grown tree between its antlers; How his horse was chopped in half by a portcullis; and my favourite about the men in the moon who slept with their tongues over their eyes because they had no lids, but could take an eye out and hold it to look for things under the bed.

Daddy said imagination was a precious gift and without it there would be no books or paintings or plays, but you have to know when to stop. 'Like the Faraway Tree?' I said. 'If you aren't careful you get stuck?'

### *Pills and puppets.*

My mother could always find a project to keep her busy. She made our clothes, (and Granny's), conjured meals out of almost nothing, and involved us in all kinds of crafts, especially close to Christmas. This year we made trinket trays from Barbola Paste and shells, glazing them with clear nail-varnish. We also made puppets.

Our school PTA, planned a glove-puppet Nativity Play. Other families made shepherds, and angels, and the Holy Family. We made kings. The heads were papier-mâché moulded round old light-bulbs. We painted their faces and beards and dried them on the mantelpiece while we made their crowns and bodies. We cut. Mummy sewed. We learned our words.

But Mummy wasn't well. She had a cough and got pills from Dr Davey. The bottle stood on the mantlepiece beside the kings' heads. It had a label with her name. I was a bit miffed. My madness pills didn't have my name on, and without thinking, I asked Daddy why.

'What pills?' he said.

I back-pedalled furiously. 'They're only for me,' I said, 'For my madness; so I don't hurt anyone.'

Daddy looked puzzled.

'It's *real* medicine,' I said, 'We get it at the chemist's.'

'... and it doesn't have your name. Does it say anything at all?'

'There's a long word but I don't know how to say it.'

'Show me.'

I rummaged behind the cutlery tray and handed him the bottle.

Daddy said, 'Pottassium Bromide.'

He looked cross. I thought he might shout. Mummy wasn't around for him to shout at so it would be me, but he just said, 'You are not mad ... and nor am I.'

(*He knew! He knew!*) I said, 'I'm sorry, Daddy.'

He said, 'It's all right. I'm not going to ask.'

(*How did he know what I was thinking?*)

Later there was an almighty row. My father threw the pills in the fire. Mummy threw the kings' heads after them and we had to make them again. But there were no more pills, for me, or Daddy, and the second lot of kings was better than the first.

# Sixteen

I went with Daddy to deliver a present to his friend Max who was with him in the RAF. He lived in a big house with a tall thin wife who smoked cigarettes in a holder. Their hall was big as a room, with double-doors to the lounge.

### *Dead beasts and door panels*

Attracted by a Christmas tree, I ran into the room and caught my toe in the mouth of a tiger that was spread-eagled on the floor. Dead animals, I thought, as I struggled to my feet. That meant they were posh. There were dead animals on the walls too, a rhino, and a giant cow with horns that met in the middle.

I realised quite quickly that Daddy was showing me off. Max produced a pack of cards called Lexicon and asked me to make a word of eight or more letters. I wrote 'APARTHEID'.

'I learned to spell it while I was ill,' I said, 'It was in the paper. It's when black people can't use the same toilets.'

Max said, 'Good Lord!'

Daddy asked Max if he knew any schools for gifted girls for when I was older; something within our means or with a scholarship. I didn't know what that meant but I wrote it down later anyway. They talked a lot of RAF talk and were very cheery. It was dark and frosty as we walked home.

It was dark and frosty too, a few days later as Daniel and I walked home from the school bus. The front door was on the latch and the hall in darkness as we hung up our coats. There was shouting from beyond. We thought we might sit on the bottom stair for a bit until they'd finished.

Suddenly there was a bang and the hall flooded with light as Daddy's arm came through the top panel of the door. One of the planks was sticking straight out, and beyond the hole was Daddy's face wearing a sheepish grin.

'Oh hello!' he said.

Mummy was completely silent.

Daddy extracted his arm from the door and put plasters on his knuckles, and Mummy served tea as if nothing had happened.

After that we listened to Children's Hour while Daddy got to work on the door with Plastic Wood. I had a list of useful things you needed when you were grown up, like a Cycle Repair Kit, Leichner Makeup Remover, invisible ink, and Gordon Moore's toothpaste to tint your gums. I added Plastic Wood when I'd got a minute.

I wondered what a gifted girl was. Daniel was adopted so I reckoned that was when you went to the Children's Home and fetched a baby and 'gifted' was when they brought the baby to *you*. But how did that fit in with 'taking after' people and things being 'in the blood'? Too complicated.

### *Revelation*

Christmas was surprisingly good. We had more trains and a crowd of metal cowboys and Indians complete with horses, a few tepees and some fence, to go with our knights in armour and American Marines. It made for some curious interactions.

Grannie Innes sent me a full-sized baby doll with soft rubber skin, and we had our first teddy bears, identical but for the ribbons round their necks. Mummy called mine Leslie after her father. Daniel said his was Margaret, though we never knew why. Granny worked her usual miracle and the cake was a train with a tender full of marzipan toys.

On Boxing Day we had games at home. There was a treasure hunt for chocolates. We played dominos, and Happy Families (yes really). Finally Daddy set up a game to guess things blindfold from their smell. The items were on cotton wool in jars; lavender polish, nutmeg, a piece of rubber, orange peel etc. Daddy brought each jar separately from the kitchen on a tin tray. Mummy wrote down our answers. I knew the last one at once. It was the stuff for the Rybar Inhaler.

There was a clang as the tray hit the floor and Daddy said 'Christ!' which was really naughty.

I pulled off the blindfold. The jar was still in my hand. Phew! I put the lid back on as Daddy took Mummy's arm and propelled her into the scullery.

I don't know what they said because Daniel was crying and I took him to play with the cowboys. In fact I don't remember tea-time or bed-time. The day just stopped dead. Years later when I realised what had happened, I thought perhaps it was chloroform or ether, but putting my mind to it I think it was Thawpit Spot Cleaner.

### *1951: Staying safe.*

After all the Christmas drama there were no more 'madness pills' and no more inhalers. My ‘eczema’ and tummy-aches disappeared, but I worried that my madness might start to show, and kept a careful check on myself in case I did something I couldn't control. As Mummy said, I didn't want to hurt anyone, did I?

At school I kept to the bike-shelter, writing poems in my notebook, watching everyone else. I checked my hands, my feet, constantly to be sure they were how I last placed them. Granny told me I must play, and bought me a skipping-rope. Mummy confiscated it and said it was dangerous. She had a row with Granny.

At least we were allowed into the playroom again. We set up the clockwork trains and all the lead figures. We arranged a pow-wow between the cowboys and the Indians who agreed to fight together against King Arthur's knights who were supported by US marines with heavy artillery.

We moved train-loads of horses and heavy guns from one end of the room to the other and set our battles on American soil. Having mastered my jigsaw of English counties I had one of American States now. The Children's Encyclopedia helped with terrain.

For a while my mother took to waking us in the night, placing our arms outside the bedclothes, sniffing our hands to be sure we hadn't touched ourselves. I worried. I slept on my back, gripping the rails of my bed-head. At Granny's the bed had nothing to grip but when I mentioned it there was another row and I stopped telling her things that Mummy did.

I just wanted people to be kind to each other. I asked God to fix it but He was too busy. At times I wished they would send me to live in hospital with Cousin Pat, and just get it over with. I didn't mind if she had fits. I didn't mind if she wet herself. She was big and warm like Granny Soal. I could bury my face in her soft cloud of hair and feel safe.

Early in February a parcel of books arrived from Birmingham, books that Pat no longer needed. I still have "The House at Pooh Corner".

'Why doesn't Pat want them now?' I asked.

'Because she's dead.' said Mummy brusquely. It was a blessing, she said. There was no future for such people.

It was decades before I knew how it happened. Pat's seizures always threw her sideways with great force. On 2nd February 1951, she had one in the hospital loo, hit the wall beside her and broke her neck. She died instantly. She was sixteen.

I wondered if I might die soon too. Granny said of course not, and anyway it was up to God. Since it was in His hands I told Him I didn't mind either way, but please could it not hurt too much. Meanwhile I promised Him I'd do my dancing and singing and acting so that Mummy could be happy making me famous.

Mummy was rehearsing a new play for CADS. "The Young Mrs Barrington". She was props and wardrobe, and Mrs Porter, the charlady. Character parts were her great skill. She could turn herself into anything she pleased, and in later life did so in quite devious ways. For Mrs Porter she had just five lines. The rest was timing and gesture. I watched and learned.

I was still dancing at Miss Thorogood's but Mummy taught me acting at home, and I heard the magic words Italia Conti and RADA. This, Mummy said, was where I could go to school in a few years if I practised my faces and voices and learned my pieces for audition.

I told Granny it wouldn't be so bad living in hospital if Mummy took me to my performances and stopped me doing anything mad. She asked Mummy what on earth she was filling my head with, and I thought perhaps she didn't approve of actors. Sometimes Granny told me I wasn't mad, but I thought she was just being kind.

### *B is for Bastard*

Some kind of treat was being planned. It was our habit at night, when voices were raised downstairs, to sit side by side on the top stair and listen. Mummy was laying down the law about it as usual. We whispered in the darkness.

Mummy said she wasn't taking Daniel. He asked me what he'd done wrong. Had he been naughty? Was it his stammer? We heard Mummy say he was "another woman's bastard." and Daniel said, 'What's a bastard?' I didn't know.

They'd be at it for a while yet, so we snuck along to Daddy's room. The Oxford Dictionary ...

*Bastard:* born out of wedlock ... erm ...

I leafed through to W

*Wedlock:* Holy matrimony.

We gave up.

I was annoyed. A seed of noble protest grew in my breast. I wasn't having Daniel left out when he'd done nothing wrong. I pictured the drama. I would be like Violet Elizabeth in the Just William stories. I'd refuse to put on my coat. I would cling to the banisters. And I'd "thkweem and thkweem till I made mythelf thick."

'I won't go either,' I whispered, 'They'll have to drag me. They can go out on their own. I'll stay at home with you?' I put my arm round him, which wasn't usually allowed. I gave him a hug and we crept back to our beds.

### *Speech and Drama*

I enjoyed my acting lessons with Mummy and learned short pieces from Shakespeare and Shaw; The Tempest, Pygmalion. There were poems too; The Listeners, The Way Through The Woods. Granny said it was too advanced for an eight-year-old, but I loved it. I read all the poetry I could find whether I understood it or not.

For diction we did The Windhover. I loved the way the sounds rolled round my mouth while my mind fell into a big feather-bed of images where the grammar and the rhymes didn't matter. I wished I could write like that.

Christina Rossetti was difficult. "Remember Me." I couldn't say the last two lines. I kept thinking of Pat. I cried.

Mummy said 'If you're going to act, young lady, you'll have to say your lines even when you're heart is breaking.'

I wept with frustration. 'It's breaking NOW!'

Granny said 'Stop it, Win! STOP IT!' and I buried my face in her dress.

This was a new sort of crying, I thought. Not the sort that tells someone you've grazed your knee, or the sort that wants something. This sort of crying happened on its own, from inside, and it hurt.

I sat cross-legged in front of the wardrobe mirror, and said it again and again. *'Better by far you should forget and smile, than that you should remember and be sad.'* and in the end I managed it without tears.

Faces were easier. We practised happy faces, sweet faces, thoughtful ones, loving ones and ones from Mummy's film magazines; Queen Elizabeth at Tilbury; Joan of Arc. Mummy was pleased and that meant everything.

There *was* a treat. It was a photo shoot and Daniel wasn't left out. We sat for Polyphotos, sheets of forty-eight contacts, the best shots selected for enlargement. Daniel brought his teddy bear, and Granny came for someone to smile at. I went first so that Daniel wouldn't be scared.

I did lots of faces, while Mummy issued orders; looking at Daniel, looking at Granny, smiling, thinking.

'Sad one!' barked Mummy, 'Think about Pat!'

Not likely! It was a horrible idea. She wanted me to cry. I set my jaw.

The first Joan of Arc shot was not saintly enough.

'They're burning you at the stake, for heaven's sake!' said Mummy, 'Look up and see Jesus coming for you.'

The photographer looked at her in disbelief, but the shot was just fine. After that it was a breeze for Daniel. He just cuddled his bear and smiled at Granny and me.

Polyphotos were a wonderful system, and a skilled operator could get good responses from babies to Grandads. They were affordable, high quality and studio-lit. There seems nothing like it today.

## *Bewilderment*

We knew Mummy was upset that Sunshine & Smiles would not be back this year, and she missed her friends at the theatre. It wasn't Daddy's fault.

Breakfasts were still a nightmare. Every move we made was a sign of some inherent evil, or a plot against her. As ever Mummy claimed that Robert Donat was twice the man Daddy was.

He must be pretty huge, we thought, because Daddy was six foot three.

If it wasn't Robert Donat it was Bunny Baron. Daddy made a joke of it. One morning he put on his best American accent,

'It's somethin' ter tell the little'uns. Ah remember yer great-ant Winnie. Ran off after a red-nose comic from a seaside Pierrot troupe.'

Mummy rolled up her Womans Own, smacked him with it, and flounced out. Daddy laid his head on his arms and laughed. He snorted and growled. His shoulders shook. It went on longer than it should. It worried me ... but grown-ups didn't cry ... did they?

I wrote it in my notebook to think about later.

On the Sunday after the photo shoot, Daniel went off after church with Mr Oakley, his class teacher. He disappeared round the side of the church clutching his teddy bear and Mr Oakley's hand. We went to Granny's for lunch. Daddy didn't come.

I asked about Daniel over lunch and Mummy said we were not to mention him any more ... to anyone ... ever. I took a breath to speak but Granny shook her head at me and I held my tongue. I asked her privately later and she said she was forbidden to speak of him too, and it was more than her life was worth. So I didn't speak of Daniel. I couldn't, there was such a stony weight in my chest.

I saw him on Monday morning at school, arriving with the children from Katherine Alderton House, the children's home. I sat in the bike-shelter as usual. They crossed my playground, two by two, in a line. I caught his eye. I waved.

He waved back. They disappeared through the green door in the wall to the other yard.

All through that week I snatched a glimpse of Daniel in the mornings, and a wave if I could catch his eye. Then someone caught his wrist and stopped him. The next week someone walked between us, keeping him close, glancing at me in case I made a dash for him. I thought about it. I was outraged. It couldn't go on. I was his sister. I was there to protect him. Something had to be done.

### *Crying in the wilderness.*

In class I asked to be excused, and as I crossed the great polished assembly hall I didn't dance and spin as I usually did when I had it to myself. Mr Oakley was also a house-father at the home. I walked straight to his classroom door. I knocked. 'Excuse me, Mr Oakley. May I see my brother.'

And Mr Oakley said, 'You don't have a brother.' and shut the door in my face.

I was paralysed for a second, then purposeful. It wasn't fair, and the world needed to know it. I walked to the centre of the great shiny hall. I looked up at the window above the dais. I took my deepest breath and let out the loudest longest wail I could muster. I challenged them all. Ignore *that* if you can!

By the time I ran out of air, every classroom door was open. Someone snatched me up and carried me to the head's office. Miss Ault was in a difficult position. My parents were part of the local teaching community. She sat me on her knee, held me, let me cry and lent me her hanky. Whatever she knew or suspected, there was nothing she could say.

### *Books*

Daddy had been ignoring me lately, but now we were talking again, mostly about books. He tested me on what books were essential. I wrote a list, and he added the ones I missed. Dictionary; thesaurus; Fowler's English Usage; Bible; encyclopedia; a dictionary of quotations; and if possible a dictionary of phrase and fable; and Observer books on flowers, birds and insects. He had all these books and more.

He took me to the library and showed me that if I ever found myself without books this was where I could look at them.

'It's called a Reference Library. They might think you should be in the children's part, but take them a leaf or a flower and ask what it is in Latin. That'll tickle their whiskers.'

He laughed. I thought we had enough books at home.

I didn't mention Daniel. I wasn't sure how he would react. The breakfast incident had disturbed me. It was a terrible sound and not like laughter at all. I was pretty sure I'd seen a man cry. I didn't know what to do, so I asked about Mr Ghandi, and apartheid, and nationalisation (my longest word to date) and why there had to be Parties.

Daddy said that if everyone could be kind and polite to each other, and not take more than they needed, we wouldn't need any of that. Maybe it would happen one day but it had to start with each person on their own. I mentioned this to Granny and she said I was 'deep', whatever that meant.

Meanwhile Mummy played her charlady part in "The Young Mrs Barrington", and brought the house down. I wished she had more parts like that. She'd be a nicer Mummy then.

### *A change of sand.*

The Easter holidays were bleak. There were no outings and I didn't want to play. Daddy helped me pack up the cowboys and Indians, and the US Marines. We took the knights off their horses and used matchsticks to mend some who had lost their heads. I tried to look forward to a trip to Margate with Granny after Easter but although she played Sorry and Snakes and Ladders with me it wasn't fun any more without Daniel.

Granny didn't come to Margate after all. Mummy and I went on our own. We stayed with a Mr Paye. There was only a single bed and I slept curled up in an old leather chair by the window.

Margate seemed livelier than Clacton. The flowerbeds were lovely. Mummy was cheerful, but there were people missing and I just wanted to go home.

But we weren't going home. Mummy told me after a few days. We would be living in Margate. I was starting school next week.

'What about Daddy?' I said.

'We forget about Daddy. We forget about Daniel. We don't mention them to anyone here. They do *not* exist. Do you understand?'

I did *not* understand. Not at all.

'What about Grannie and Grandad in Birmingham?'

'You'll not see *them* again, and anyway Grandad Innes is dead.'

'What? Like Pat?'

'He had a heart attack.'

It was the last straw. There was a big round cushion on the bed. I hurled my face into the middle of its faded cover and howled.

'Such a fuss about a mad old man.' said Mummy.

When I calmed down we went for a walk east of the pier. We came to the Cliftonville Lido where the great white walls of a swimming pool towered over the beach. There was a whole complex with amusements and cafes and entertainment. We stopped by the theatre to look at the bill-board. It said "Sunshine & Smiles".

'Oh look!' Mummy said 'Uncle Bunny's here!'

I looked at the poster. I looked at Mummy. I was eight years old. I wasn't born yesterday.

# *Part Three*

# *Margate*

# *Seventeen*

It's not that my mother had affairs. She had obsessions. Many were lifelong and ran in parallel with others. All of them were men who did not respond; and woe betide anyone who did.

Around her chief idols, my mother wove tales of intrigue and hopeless love to which she could only respond with friendship. She pursued each man relentlessly, infiltrating his life with helpfulness, cake, and an air of untouchable respectability. Those that I met were always kind to me.

There was the actor Robert Donat, the comedian Bunny Baron, and in the 1960s Stan West, the courier from an Italian coach tour, who she claimed was her colleague in MI5.

There were others, names from her youth that made Granny tut and throw up her hands, and new imagined suitors who failed the test of purity.

Sometimes she played the femme fatale, pursuing, flirting and stalking someone obsessively until she got a response. An attempted kiss branded him a 'dirty beast' and the guillotine of her scorn descended. Another head in the basket. Outright rejection was also inadvisable.

Despite her oddities, my mother was a skilled teacher, and secured a post in Ramsgate. I was enrolled at Salmestone Primary in Margate and to my delight I found that I was Elizabeth again. I had been Mary since 1947, with all its confusions, but now I had my old Birmingham name back, the one Granny called me, and Daddy.

Daddy.

I tried not to think about him.

I was at Salmestone for three years, the last settled period of schooling I had. I am forever grateful. I remembered little of lessons in Clacton, but Salmestone encouraged me, inspired me, and even understood me. I was precocious and way ahead of everyone else. It can't have been easy.

At Salmestone our artwork on the walls was neatly displayed, not just bunged up with a drawing pin. Lessons were interesting and varied. And there was singing.

We sat cross-legged on the floor of the assembly hall, under the big light windows. We sang folk-songs, "Turpin Hero", "Henry Martin", and girls dressing up as soldiers. The teacher sang "Sweet Polly Oliver" and handed out sheets of words. It was my kind of music. The kind my parents sang.

I made friends at Salmestone too. Terry, whose Dad was a wrestler, and Mandy whose builder father had a sign by his door, backed by a long crack in the brickwork. There was Philip, small and shy, but always up for an adventure, and Malcolm, who made me laugh, but talked of deep things and sometimes held my hand. I spent hours with one or more of them every day, and though our eventual parting was sudden and complete, they were real chums and I never forgot them.

### *Aye-aye Cap'n!*

We lived in the Ramsgate Road. Mr Paye, our landlord was an old sailor, his tattoos crinkled and vague on his sinewy arms. Born around 1880, Mr Paye began his career on sailing barges, and joined the Navy before WW1.

Mummy was usually out, so I spent a lot of time with him in his kitchen. If he knew he was being used as a baby-sitter he never complained. He was full of stories, and some nights he played his harmonica to make the dog howl. He made me cocoa, but always sent me to bed on time.

Mr Paye's kitchen door led onto a high deck with a stair to the garden. Beneath it doors led under the house to storerooms full of bottled fruit, and crocks of eggs preserved in isinglass.

The garden stretched all the way to the street behind. There were chickens, and fruit trees, and all manner of vegetables. He made me a plot of my own, about ten feet square. He dug, I followed, picking out the slippery lumps of chalk, and when we'd got a tilth he showed me how to sow carrots, and peas, and radishes, like the ones we had in Birmingham when I was little. I wanted to tell him about that, but I'd have to speak about people I mustn't mention.

Margate was vibrant where Clacton had been sedate, but Margate had an extra ingredient. Americans. USAAF Manston was just outside town and the airmen diluted our buttoned-up Englishness with their warmth. They smiled at people. They said 'Hi!' They called old ladies 'Maam'.

Americans had looser limbs. They walked with a swing. At school everybody's big sister wanted one for her very own, and everybody's Dad said 'No!'

There were always a few Americans in the Greek Cypriot café on the sea-front where we often ate. Food was still rationed so the choice was limited. Most things were on toast; beans, sardines, herring roe. There were no fried eggs or omelets, but there was soup, and to really push the boat out, a Vienna Steak, or a real sausage with mash and tinned peas.

The café had atmosphere. It was a family business. Mamma and Pappa, their extended family, and their children. Maria, was fourteen and treated me like a sister. Antonio was my age and Theodore was four. They fussed around the customers. They recognised every face. It was the ideal spot for boys three thousand miles from home.

I went to the café if I couldn't find Mummy. She was either there, or turned up later. Sometimes it felt like home. It was where I got my hugs.

'Poor thing! She starvin'. Wess yo mamma?' and a toasted tea cake appeared.

'I can't take it. I'd better wait until Mummy comes.'

'It's on the house. You give, you gonna receive OK? So maybe I win the pools.'

I wondered if they could adopt me.

### *Familiar faces*

Reconnected with "Sunshine & Smiles" my mother lost interest in my faults for a while. There was no more talk of madness, which was good, but there was no more dancing or singing either. I missed that.

The Cliftonville Lido was a complex, a vision in cream with red roofs and paintwork, and built on several levels. A ratcheted cabin carried less able folks up from the pool.

If Mummy wasn't at the café she was at the Lido theatre. I had the run of the place as I had at the Westcliffe. All the familiar faces were there, Iris Villiers and Johnny Peresino the singers, Tom Katz and the Saxophone Six, and, joy of joys, Chuck O'Neil and Billy Nelson.

When they saw me they were surprised, but lit up in the way Granny always did.

'If it isn't Mary-Mary!' they said, 'Don't be contrary, Mary. Tell us why you're here.'

'We live here now,' I said, 'and I'm not Mary any more. I'm Elizabeth. That's my *real* name."

'We like that, don't we William? We shall call you Libba for short,' said Chuck, 'Where's your Mum, anyway? Where's Mrs Trouble?'

That was a bit rude, but stage people had their own way of talking. They teased and acted out. The rudeness was part of the fun. Mummy said Chuck and Billy were 'fairies' but I didn't see how that was a problem. I don't know if Chuck and Billy were gay, but they were certainly very camp.

Mummy took me to another theatre to see "This Was The Army" where all the men dressed as ladies. The one who sold us a program wore an evening gown and looked like Lauren Bacall. Another wore a crinoline and sang, sitting on a swing entwined with flowers.

I told Chuck and Billy where we'd been and Chuck said 'Ooh! We don't mix with them. They're rough! *Really* rough!"

Well I thought they were beautiful.

I took Chuck and Billy as I found them, though children did know there were people to avoid. The ones grown-ups said might 'like that sort of thing' which presumably meant something rude. We had a sixth sense about them.

One of these was our class teacher. I only had him for one term. There was no problem with his lessons, mostly spelling bees and drawing; a jug, a brush and a packet of soap powder arranged on a chair. And I did learn to sharpen a pencil with a razor blade.

This teacher enjoyed spanking people with gym shoes, but only girls. He always sat sideways with them over his knee so that we could see their knickers. He leered at the class wanting the boys to snigger. One or two did, but they were the rough boys. We didn't play with them.

Terry always looked down at his desk. Malcolm and Philip closed their eyes. We knew he was strange. Terry said 'Maybe he likes that sort of thing.'

There! Just as I thought.

### *The water is wide.*

It was good to see old faces at the Lido and make new friends at school. And it was good to feel welcome at the café, but I missed my family. I looked out to sea, northward across the great estuary, and knew that Clacton was somewhere there, maybe around the one o'clock direction. Daddy was there, and Granny, and Daniel, going to our school as usual. I hoped the home was being kind to him and not letting his shoes get too tight.

Sometimes I walked to the end of the pier so that I felt a little closer. I let the wind roar in my ears and cut out everything else. I was puzzled. Why did Mummy take us both for photos and send Daniel away in days? Was this what we overheard on the stairs? ... 'not taking Daniel.' ... nothing to do with a treat at all.

Towards the end of term we sat for the annual school photographs. The teachers said I was a mess. They were right. Mummy had lost interest in my appearance as well as my madness. My hair was wispy and my blouse unironed. Thank goodness they couldn't see what was under the tunic.

On July 10th I was nine and was to meet Mummy at the cafe for a treat. I went straight from school. Pappa gave me a card from everyone. I waited. And I waited. After an hour I put on my cardigan to walk home.

'You can't go!' Mamma shouted, 'You gotta have a birthday!' She looked me up and down. 'Come on, I press you blouse.'

Shouting something at the family in Greek, she led me up the stairs and divested me of my tunic. Oh dear! There were no buttons on my blouse below the collar and my vest was full of holes. She did her best. She found a silky kerchief to tie round my neck. She brushed my hair. Maria braided it and lent two hair-slides.

'*Now* you havin' a birthday.' said Mamma.

They fed me mushrooms on toast, a luxury item, and tinned peaches with ice-cream. The Americans sang Happy Birthday. I was just tackling a piece of cherry fruit-cake when Mummy breezed in, immaculately dressed, and showered everyone with gratitude, hoping I hadn't been a nuisance.

'She been a angel.' said Mamma, following up with some high-speed Greek with eye-rolling.

'Thank goodness Mamma didn't say that in English.' Maria whispered as Mummy paid at the counter. 'I tell you later.'

Apparently it was something about the Bad Fairy.

### *I-spy adventure.*

I had friends now. Not just Granny letting me play with Eunice Ibbot in Clacton when Mummy wasn't looking, but real friends. The five of us were all heavily into I-Spy. We filled in our books of birds or flowers or railway things, had them signed by an adult, and sent them off to Big Chief I-Spy for a badge.

One Saturday towards the end of term when Terry, Mandy and Malcolm were unavailable and the Infamous Five were reduced to the Bored Two, Philip Newberry and I did a tree hunt. He knew where there were lots of different ones round a big empty house on the edge of town, an old hospital he thought. We squeezed through a shrubbery and scoured the perimeter for rare specimens. We could come back later 'officially' with an adult and our books.

After a while we ran across the lawns and explored outside the house. We found an open trapdoor with a slide. Irresistible! We slid. It was a coal-cellar, mostly full of coke, but the slide was fun. 'Let's do it again!' ... but the only way out was back up the coal-chute.

Philip was smaller and slighter than I, and couldn't get a grip on the sides. We thought we were stuck, but I put my head under his bottom and shoved him up ahead of me. Gosh, that was close. Better not do it again. We looked at each other. We were *filthy*!

Philip went home to get clean. I didn't dare. My dress was covered in coal-dust. I wandered down to the beach, the quiet part east of the pier. I walked into the sea and sat down. I rolled about a bit. I found a rock-pool and washed my face and arms and watched the little crabs running away.

The sun was hot. I ran up and down for a while and when my dress was dry enough I walked back to Ramsgate Road. My wet sandals rubbed my feet and I was glad to get there. Mummy was out, so I had tea and toast with Mr Paye and went to bed. The grubby dress would go to the laundry. I was clean. Mummy would never notice. I was wrong!

Since we first lived with Mr Paye, we had taken a second room, upstairs where my mother and I shared a double bed. When she woke me the morning after the tree-hunt she said 'What's this?' The centre of my pillow was grey.

'I'm sorry, Mummy, I fell in a coal-hole. I thought I got clean in the sea.'

She pulled back the covers. All around my feet was grey too. There was coal ingrained behind my heels and black deposits between my toes.

'We were looking for trees for Big Chief I-Spy.'

'Did you find any?' (*Why wasn't she angry?)*

'Lots, but we didn't have our books.'

'Then you'd better show me,' said Mummy, 'but first we're going to get clean.'

I never knew why she wasn't angry, but all that day she was the Mummy I wished I had; like a special day out.

We had use of Mr Paye's bathroom only for teeth and strip-washes, so I hadn't had a soak since April. Mummy curled up her hair, tied a scarf round it, and we went to the Public Baths.

"Slipper Baths" it said outside, with a list of prices. A wide lady in a white overall issued us a scratchy towel and a mean piece of soap. I thought she looked like Hermann Goering.

'You can only 'ave the one towel,' she said, 'And if you're doing your 'air, clean the plug'ole.'

Mummy said 'Naturally!' and took off her white lace gloves.

The cubicle had a grey terrazzo floor and white tiled walls with dirty grout ... and the biggest deepest bath I had ever seen. There was an old soap-box to help you climb over the side. We sat at opposite ends, as Daniel and I used to do, laughing and playing with the soap. Mummy had brought her Lux.

The miserable walls disappeared in steam. She produced a loofah and pumice stone, and Bristowe's Lanolin Shampoo, a powder you mixed with water. She washed my hair. There was coal-dust on the bubbles.

Back at Ramsgate Road, in a clean frock and undies, we made sandwiches and washed some of the radishes and carrots I'd grown in Mr Paye's garden. We took them out to the old hospital with my I-Spy book and I showed Mummy the trees.

She showed me how to find others; what to look for on the ground; leaves that grow opposite or alternately, patterns in bark. And I found new trees, hornbeam and white beam, wild service tree and guelder rose, using my book and what she taught me.

We ate sitting on the cliff-top and I was so happy I kept wanting to cry. Maybe she liked me after all.

### *Sleepy baby.*

Mummy had a free pass for the Lido Theatre and we spent many evenings there. I often slept in my seat, waking on fine nights when the roof slid open and cool air hit my face. On the stage Iris and Johnny sang “Loveliest Night of the Year” while the audience looked up at the stars. Bedtimes were forgotten. I nodded off in dressing-rooms while Mummy talked to her friends. We walked home late and I fell into bed.

After school broke up for the summer, Mummy spent days at the theatre and I spent more time alone. I roamed the beach among the crowds, and the sea-front amusement halls, lurking by juke-boxes, singing along and being chased out into the sunshine. Judy Garland was telling us to “Get Happy” but mostly I wanted rest. I was so tired. Sometimes I just lay on the sand and slept.

The sea-front was a community from the clock-tower to Dreamland, and I was being watched unawares. Word got back to the café that I'd been seen sleeping under the pier and they sent Andros to find me. He was a cousin or nephew who waited tables, a man in my eyes, but probably only eighteen. 'Mamma says come.' he said.

She put a bowl of soup in front of me, and a buttered roll.

'I haven't enough pocket money for this,' I said, 'Can I wash dishes to pay for it like they do in films?'

Mamma had a minor Greek explosion after which she said, 'Tell you what. You can help Maria fold the cloths.' and so I did.

Maria fed them into the rotary iron and I piled them up with the napkins and tea-towels, in a little room at the top. From the flat roof we looked out to sea one way and into the Dreamland Funfair behind. Music played, the smell of hot sugar drifted up from the candy spinners, and the crowds squealed on the rides. It was the British seaside at its best.

# *Eighteen*

There were rhythms to summer in a seaside town. They mixed and merged. They swept over and under each other, interlocking sometimes for a week, or an hour, orchestrated by nature, and opposed by humans who would bend them to their will. Nature always won.

Seaside landladies had rules. In B&Bs and guesthouses they were tacked to walls in dining rooms, and the backs of bedroom doors. The greatest of these commandments was *"Thou shalt not enter the house between 10am and 5pm."*

Families saved all year, arriving with battered luggage and fractious children to make the best of a precious week. If it was wet they spent much of it sitting in cliff-top shelters, macs flapping, trying to eat their chips before they were cold. Guests in the better hotels watched them from comfortable sunrooms, and wished they would go away. Class and income were all.

### *Time and tide*

For the most part, however, the sun shone, and the rhythm of the landladies interlocked with the rhythm of the sea. Tides were a little later each day and when high tides were early and late, the beach was crowded all day. But as they crept forward, a high tide at noon pushed everyone up onto the sea-front, crowding the cafes and amusement arcades, and the entertainments on the pier.

Each cycle fell later in the week and when a low-tide day fell on Saturday we had the beach almost to ourselves as visitors went home and the landladies changed the bed-linen.

I watched the tide-table by the harbour, made notes in my book, and tried to predict the next 'big beach' days. It had something to do with the moon, I guessed. I asked Mr Paye. He'd been a sailor. He thought I was too young to understand, but when I showed him my notes he told me how the earth stretched and shrank. 'Like it's breathing,' he said, 'but real slow like.'

The world breathed! It changed everything. It wasn't just a tin globe on Daddy's desk. It was *alive*! I stood at the edge of the water and wished my arms were long enough to hug it.

### *Secrets and lies*

Chuck and Billy were from Manchester, quite old in my eyes, and had been to Hollywood before the war and made films. While my tap-shoes still fitted I took them down to the theatre sometimes and Chuck watched me do my steps, as he had in Clacton. I hoped to have lessons again, though I never did.

At the Lido Mummy was possibly moonlighting in wardrobe as she was forever about the place, refitting costumes and helping with hair. I quickly found I was expected to join a conspiracy to head Mummy off and give Bunny some peace.

'Doesn't Bunny like her then?' I asked.

'Oh no,' said Chuck, 'She's a godsend, your Mum. She's just a bit *keen*.'

I thought I knew what he meant. Bossy maybe?

'Yes, *keen*,' said Chuck, 'but she's had a hard life. She's safe here. Your Dad can't hurt you now.'

My reaction shocked him.

'Daddy's *never* hurt us. She didn't run away from him. She just followed "Sunshine and Smiles" because she wants to be in the theatre. She wants to be near Bunny Baron. Daddy CRIED!'

'Ssshhh! Oh Lordy-Lordy!'

Chuck said he needed some fresh air and Billy came with us to the beach. I sat between them on the sand with a small vanilla cone.

'Come on! Tell!"

'I'm telling tales on Mummy,' I said, 'My tongue will come out in spots.'

'No, that's if you tell lies, so tell the truth and all will be well.'

I didn't say much more. I told them about Daniel and how I wasn't to mention him. I didn't mention the madness.

'Please don't tell Mummy I said anything.'

'Not ... a ... word.' they said, and I don't think they ever did.

### *Name that tune*

Margate radiated from a spot near the clock tower. Shopping streets ran uphill and inland. Eastward the posh end of the promenade ran past the Winter Garden and big hotels to the Lido at Cliftonville. But westward, from the clock to the Dreamland Cinema, the seafront was a strip of cafes, photo-shops, kiosks and amusement arcades facing onto the sands.

Each arcade had a juke box. Each played a different song as I passed. There was no 'Top Ten', no 'play list'. The variety was enormous; Mario Lanza, Bing Crosby, Frankie Laine. Rosemary Cloony wanted people to "Come on a my house" Somebody else "Tawt he tawd a puddy-tat" and Nat King Cole was "Unforgettable".

Then one day I heard something different, something that didn't make sense at first. The opening bars swung up and down ...

One two three FOUR (up)

One two three FOUR (down)

One two three FOUR (up a bit higher)

ONE two three four FIVE (running down)

I couldn't get it out of my head. I asked one of the Tom Katz Saxophone Six and hummed him the first bit.

'Like this?' he said, picking up his sax. I got goose bumps. I still do. 'Stardust,' he said, 'It's by Hoagy Carmichael.'

Now there's a name you don't forget in a hurry.

### *North by north-west.*

Out beyond Cliftonville there were soldiers sometimes. Just three or four, on the grass above the cliffs, with a field telephone and the world's worst sandwiches, all thick white bread and meagre fillings.

They looked out to sea a lot so I asked them where Clacton was so that I could send 'thinks' to Granny, and

Daddy, and Daniel. They had a compass, but weren't allowed to show me their map. I wandered sadly home.

*Why* didn't Mummy have any books?

BOOKS!

Of course! Daddy told me before we left: where to find books. He *knew*!

I dug out my geometry set and asked a policeman the way to the library, where I got the expected response. They showed me the Children's Library, a mess of dog-eared Blyton and Beacon Readers.

'Excuse me. I need to see a map of England.' I put my protractor down on the counter as sign I was serious. A map was found.

Clacton wasn't around one-o-clock as I thought, but a couple of degrees west of north. That was all I needed. I carried my protractor with me after that. I found North from the weather vanes on the sea-front. I set my protractor on my lap and sent thoughts and waves, two degrees to the left.

I told Andros at the café. He said Granny was too far away to see me but I reckoned God would send my wave to Granny in her sleep. 'Tell me when you dream her waving back.' he said. But I didn't dream waves from Granny. I dreamed cuddles, but then I always had.

### *Certificate A.*

My mother's earlier work in film meant that we went to the cinema often. Many of the films were Certificate A, and too grown-up for me. I didn't understand the plots. I just enjoyed the scenery, the costumes and the music.

During the summer term we had seen "Pandora And The Flying Dutchman". James Mason was intense, and Ava Gardner glamourous. There were wonderful storms at sea and a tragic drowning. I enjoyed that, but at the end something appeared that I recognised. A card, which said "The moving finger writes and having writ moves on." I knew it from one of Daddy's books.

At school the following week, our teacher asked us to write one line of a poem we liked, so I wrote that. We had to read them out. I read mine.

‘Stand up!’ Barked my teacher, the man who liked exposing little girls' knickers. ‘Say the rest of the verse.’

He was challenging me. I wasn't having it. I'd show him! Remembering my acting lessons with Mummy I struck my Joan of Arc pose and said:

*‘nor all thy piety nor wit,*
*Can lure it back to cancel half a line,*
*Nor all thy tears wash out a word of it.*
’

‘Oh!’ he said ‘We have a right little Flora Robson here.’ I didn't know who she was. I didn't know the word 'ignoramus' either which was just as well or I'd have been over his knee with my knickers on view to the boys.

### *Home and away*

In late August we visited Granny in Clacton to collect the annual knitting. It was good to be back at Skeena. The house had cedar woodwork and its own special smell that never changed. Granny didn't change either, and the food was even better. Toad-in-the-hole! And at last! Tripe and onions!

Another reason for our visit was Granny's thrice-yearly tryst with the Toni Home Perm. This did *not* smell so nice. It took hours. They sent me out for a walk.

What a stroke of luck! I didn't say, but I knew exactly where I was going; to see Daddy. I skipped along the St Osyth Road, but when I got to Ellis Road, the house was empty and up for sale. He'd gone and I didn't know where.

I walked on to Tower Road. The pictures outside the Westcliffe Theatre were of people I didn't know. Down on the sea-front there were strangers sitting outside our beach-hut. I walked up and down for a bit. No Daddy. No Daniel. I wanted to cry but I didn't want anyone to ask what was the matter.

The wind was cooler. There were dahlias on the flower stalls, and chrysanthemums. In the end I walked to the end of the pier and realised that I was lonely. I missed my friends in Margate, the school, the café, the theatre. It was over there somewhere, across the water.

I fished my protractor out of my bag. If Clacton was just west of North, Margate must be just east of south. That was fun. But I realised too, that in Clacton I missed Margate, and in Margate I would miss Clacton; like missing Birmingham too, ... and Pat ... and Grandad Innes.

Maybe you just had to enjoy being where you were. Yes, that was it; and the people too. Thus I took a big step into growing up.

### ***Barking.***

For the new school year we had a lady teacher, much to our relief. She taught me for a whole year but I only remember her as 'Miss'. She was lovely and I feel sad that I cannot remember her name.

Miss soon discovered that some of us were hunting trees and, Nature Study being one of her pet subjects, she had us doing bark rubbings in churchyards and public gardens, as the leaves began to turn. We made an impressive classroom display and learned how to spell 'chlorophyll'.

Miss's other interest was English Composition so, while harvest was ongoing she had us pestering our parents for weekend trips to see combines and balers and fruit-pickers. Then we'd to write a story around a piece of equipment.

Horrid little creatures that we were, these stories mostly entailed grisly accidents, and miracles of complex surgery. Mandy's Dad had a small piggery just outside town where Terry and I sometimes helped with feed. I had plans for a tale involving a pig-swill boiler, but Mandy said ‘Don't you dare!’

It was a shame really. I'd got a really tragic ending where the victim's fate was discovered only when the buttons of his school blazer turned up at mucking-out. As I said ... horrid little creatures, nine-year-olds!

### ***Smokes and socialism.***

Mr Paye grew his own tobacco. The leaves hung in bunches round the kitchen stove-pipe. As it grew too cold to play outside after school I sat with him at the table while he cut out the stalks and I wiped both sides of the leaves with a cloth soaked in a 'special mixture' of rum and black treacle.

He made the tobacco into rolls and whipped them with string. It smelled lovely like that, but was disgusting in his pipe.

Mr Paye didn't go to the cinema, so I told him my favourites. "The Lady With The Lamp" about Florence Nightingale was exciting, "The Tales of Hoffman", was sad, but my favourite was "Mr Drake's Duck".

Someone found his boiled egg was radioactive. Officialdom went into overdrive as various authorities claimed ownership of the duck that laid it, and the farm was hemmed in with soldiers, and civil servants.

Mr Paye said it was a send-up of all the government interference left over from the war; ID cards, rationing, and now, Mr Paye said, in spite of all his promises Mr Atlee was going to charge people for teeth and glasses to pay for a war in Korea.

He was incensed. He said Mr Churchill would be back in No. 10 very soon. He was right, and the ID cards were scrapped the next year.

Mummy took me to "Mine Own Executioner", a grim psycho-thriller, in black and white, and totally unsuitable for a child. People argued a lot. There was someone called a psychiatrist. But the image that stuck was a man on a ledge high on a building, holding a pistol to his head. I shut my eyes and put my fingers in my ears. Afterwards Mummy said he had 'blown his brains out'. He haunts me still, just standing there, waiting.

Sometimes Mummy said I would end with my brains 'all over a lavatory wall, like your cousin Pat' and for years I thought wrongly that Pat had shot herself like the man in the film.

"Sunshine and Smiles" left Margate, heading for pantomime. They would be back next year. As they packed, Mummy became upbeat and started making hearty meals at Ramsgate Road. She always included Mr Paye, who relished her cooking. "Win's Dinners" he called them, steak and kidney pudding, liver and onions, shepherd's pie, all with vegetables from his garden. Mummy beamed under his praise.

This was a kind and thoughtful Mummy, a domestic Goddess, indispensable and supportive. She made a big fuss of me when he was around and he told me how lucky I was. I felt guilty that I doubted him.

By contrast, Christmas at Clacton was bleak. Granny did her best but perhaps her heart wasn't in it. There was no novelty cake. No dressing up to hand out gifts. Last year the cake was a train and Daniel wound up his engines to bring in the Aunties' presents. He blew his whistle and waved his little flag all unaware, and I realised that Mummy knew all along what was to happen to him.

We played Monopoly and Ludo with Granny and I tried to be cheerful, but deep down I didn't want to speak to Mummy at all.

### *1952: Window dreamer*

Unknown to me, Mummy was reinventing herself as the mother of a lost child.

Our headmaster, Mr Walker, wanted a word with me about not paying attention in class. There was too much gazing out of the window and not looking at the book.

'I know it's difficult when we lose somebody, Elizabeth, but you must think how hard it is for your Mummy too. She has lost her little boy.'

I retched and swallowed. 'It isn't true!'

'What isn't?'

'I mustn't talk about them. I mustn't mention them ever again or God will be cross.'

'I'll have a word with Him about that,' said Mr Walker 'but you'd better tell me about it.'

'Mummy put Daniel in a home in Clacton. He came to school with the other children and they wouldn't let me talk to him. They said I didn't have a brother. Then we came to live here.'

Mr Walker said 'Oh dear.'

I was close to tears. I couldn't stop now. He did ask.

'I went round to our house when we were at Granny's but it's for sale and Daddy's moved and I don't know where he's gone.' I dissolved.

'So your father didn't die?'

'No! No!' I wanted to say Mummy was a liar but you had to honour your mother and father or you broke one of the commandments.

Mr Walker said 'Oh dear.' again.

Mr Walker was not Miss Ault of my old Holland Road school. He did not do hugs and lending you his hanky, and anyway I was nine now and a bit big for that. He said he was glad I'd told him, that God would understand, and that perhaps we'd talk about the day-dreaming another time; tomorrow perhaps.

# *Nineteen*

I imagine head-teachers saw situations like mine more often in the years after the war; fractured families where the only person without a hidden agenda was the child. What did these children know? What had they been told? Teachers were there to educate, not get involved, but that was almost impossible.

To me Mr Walker was distant in the way grown-up men were, but he explained and reassured, and though he stood no nonsense he was always fair, and as kind as he dared to be. I was called to his office again next day.

### *The need to know.*

Why did I leaf through the rest of the text-book instead of concentrating on the given page? Because I was looking for something new, something I hadn't done already. Maybe I'd find it further on in the book. I wasn't used to learning among other people.

'They gave me things to do on my own at Holland Road,' I said, 'I do read the page, honestly, but then I know it and I want to know some more. The books go back in the cupboard afterwards so I have to go to the library later to find out.'

'And what kind of things do you want to find out, Elizabeth?'

'I know why the moon doesn't fall down, but I want to know what it weighs. It must be tons and tons.'

I was getting into my stride.

'... and I want to know more about the planets ... and atoms. They're going to blow the world to SMITHEREENS!

'And who gave you that idea?'

'It's in the paper, and people talk about it all the time. Mr Stalin wants to kill EVERYONE in the WHOLE world.'

'Don't worry. We can leave the scientists to deal with the atoms, and anyway, girls don't do science.'

I wanted to speak out without seeming rude. I risked it. 'Madame Curie did.'

Mr Walker changed the subject. He asked me to curb my curiosity during lessons and not leaf through the books, but I could come and see him, maybe once a week, if I found out anything wonderful in the library. It was a deal.

As for what the moon weighed, I sat on the sea-front thinking that as we knew how far away it was and how fast it was going we ought to be able to work it out. I could spend happy hours just thinking about things like that, with no books at all.

### *Little white lies*

To be fair, most separated women had to tell the white lie of widowhood in order to get a job, especially in my mother's case, as a teacher. The Daniel lie was probably embroidery.

Meanwhile, the King was dead. He lay on a catafalque surrounded by white lilies and soldiers with swords. The sad princess flew home to the funeral. The black-veiled ladies slid away in their limousines leaving her to be queen, and although the nation was in mourning, there was hope and freshness. We hadn't had a queen for fifty years, nor a Queen Elizabeth for three hundred and fifty. We were to be the New Elizabethans. That felt encouraging.

The librarians were used to me by now, bringing shells and rocks and feathers for identification. They let me into the adult reference section and even helped me find books. In the art section I discovered Erte, Poiret, Morris, Rennie Mckintosh, and the wonderful Escher with his wild perspectives. I told Mr Walker. I wanted to draw streets that faded into the distance, and sure enough, Miss taught us all how to do it.

It was a busy spring. Mr Paye throve on my mother's cooking. He got new teeth on the National Health and took to smoking Park Drive cigarettes instead of his homegrown baccy. He polished the banisters and the letterbox, and sent the curtains to the cleaners, along with some clothes. Mummy said we would look after him as he grew old.

Another reason for Mummy's happiness was the Margate Operatic Society; Amateur dramatics *with* music and dance.

What could be better? This year they were doing "Rose Marie" at the Hippodrome. She signed up for wardrobe and spent the next three winters on their productions. As her assistant I had probably the most fun of my whole childhood, and learned how big productions were organised. I polished a lot of boots.

We explored back-stage at the Hippodrome. Mummy made lists and took measurements for the Rose Marie costumes. "Sunshine and Smiles" would soon be back too. By the time we went to Clacton for Easter she was bright-eyed and energised. I liked that. She was fun when she was happy.

### *A change of scene.*

Mummy was so full of joy and enthusiasm when we arrived at Granny's that she couldn't stop talking. Granny listened to her happy plans; how she was indispensible to Mr Paye, who would leave her his house in gratitude. She had little sketches of what she would do when it was hers.

When Granny could get a word in edgeways she told us that Daniel was out of the children's home and living with Daddy in Colchester. She was happy about that. So was I. Not so Mummy. There was a hissy fit.

There were times when Mummy's face shut down suddenly, and reopened upon a different scene, like the next act of a play. It did so now. She sat silent and fuming on the sofa.

Granny said, 'Meanwhile, back at the stockade ...' and went to put the kettle on. I went with her.

The rest of the holiday was dominated by plans to remove Daniel from Daddy's care. "The Authorities" would intervene. Granny said it was out of Mummy's hands, and Daniel deserved to be loved. Mummy said he was a "child of Satan" and Granny said 'Rubbish!'

They quarreled, and suddenly the Innes madness was back. Daddy was not fit to care for a child. He was insane.

'Like *that* one!' Mummy pointed at me. Granny said to leave me out of it, and Mummy suggested Pier Avenue Baptist Church might like to know she was born in the gutter. The quarrel ended abruptly.

Mummy broke the tension later, singing "Molly Malone" as they dried the dishes. It was always their sign of truce and Granny sang too. I did not know the song was a taunt, nor that Granny joined in so that I would not guess. She was indeed the daughter of an East End fishmonger and afraid of exposure and ostracism. I don't care! She'd have made ten of the rest of us anytime.

### *Little bumps. Big drama.*

I needed to talk to Granny. Something odd had happened during a sleepover with my friend Mandy. Nothing bad. Just odd. Mandy's big sister Sally was seventeen. Mandy said, 'Elizabeth's growing whiskers under her arms like yours.' I let her see.

Sally said, 'You're too young for that. You must be growing too fast.'

'I think I am,' I said, 'My chest is too fat.'

She asked if it hurt. I said it did and Sally sent for their Mum who declared that, young or not, I was growing bosoms. Oh no! Embarrassing! Mandy's Mum said that new bosoms must be looked after and I should talk to my mother.

I didn't. I waited to see Granny who confirmed that bosoms were indeed on the way. 'Win!' she said to my mother, 'Elizabeth needs a brassiere.'

Mummy didn't exactly scream 'Freak!' and flee the room, but she said 'There you are! I might have known!' and blamed it on the Inneses. Early development was a sign of decadent blood she said. It went along with the immorality and madness of epilepsy. My heart sank.

I looked at my bumps in the mirror later as I undressed for bed. My mind raced. Mummy must be right. I would start to have fits soon like cousin Pat. I'd have to live in a hospital. I didn't know how Pat died but thought she must have killed herself because she couldn't have a normal life so I wondered if I should do the same. I wrote it in my diary.

When Granny came to tuck me in I said I wished I was dead. She cried. I cried. Then she told me that maybe they were a bit early, but there was nothing wrong with my bumps, and they needed a bra. She took me out next day and bought me two!

### *Happy News.*

Back in Margate, Mr Paye looked pleased with himself. He declared he'd missed "Win's dinners" and was glad to see us. He had something to tell us after tea, he said, something we would enjoy. Mummy sang a little song as she cooked.

When the dishes were cleared Mr Paye told us that he'd been very down before we came. He'd neglected himself and the house, especially since his old shipmate Evans died. Our company had been good for him, and the wonderful meals that Mummy cooked. He needed to ensure a permanent supply of company and good cooking. So ...

... he was going to marry Mrs Evans.

I said, 'How lovely!' Mummy kicked my ankle under the table.

Mrs Evans was his shipmate's widow, and the reason for the polished furniture and new teeth. She was very sweet but Mummy declared her a gold-digger. The whole idea was disgusting, and she wasn't sharing her kitchen ... 'But it isn't your kitchen, Mummy.' I said, casually as a statement of fact.

We were gone in a week, to a bed-sit on top of The Cecil Hotel in Arthur Road, Cliftonville, very near the Lido. Mummy met me out of school and said we'd moved. I never saw Mr Paye again.

There was no time to mope in our room at the Cecil. The costumes and scenery for Rose Marie were due, and the Operatic Society went into overdrive. We prowled backstage at the Hippodrome while Mummy worked out where the wicker skips were to go in the corridors and in what order. She drew up her charts and notices and I made cards and tickets for each character, scene and member of cast.

There is nothing like the excitement of seeing the naked stage, all bare brick walls and ropes and hooks, and watching it transform. The big doors at the back opened off the street and scenery trucks queued to deliver flats and gauzes and rolls of back-drops. They smelled of paint and other theatres, and could look quite tatty close up, but that was the magic. Stand in the stalls, turn on the lights and you were in Canada; in the morning; in the evening; at night. I ran about with a chart, setting gelatins in the footlights.

Up in the Dress Circle Mummy and I pinned character tickets to the backs of seats allowing the whole centre front for the leads. Each costume change was laid out in order and items checked against invoices and Mummy's lists.

I set out the chorus further back, running up and down the stairs, checking names against sizes. The "Totem-tom-tom" chorus number involved tall hats which I could only carry one at a time. I got a lot of exercise.

The Rose Marie costumes were complicated. There were Indians, hunters, miners, men in fancy waistcoats, elegant ladies, dancers, and Mounties with brass buttons and shiny boots. Everything was checked for fit, rips, tears and missing buttons, and against a list of gloves, hats, badges, gun-belts and holsters. It took all day but eventually everything was hung in order in 'wardrobe' and Mummy set out her needles and threads and spare fixings. It was more exciting than the show itself. I was having the time of my life!

### *Drink and drivel.*

As a show, I did not like Rose Marie. At the Saturday pictures I had never liked the idea that you must shoot someone just because he was an Indian. The Totem number suggested that all Indians were drunks; and on *gin*! If they were going to be insulting they might at least be accurate.

I held forth. The problem was *whisky*, and anyway it was white people who gave it them. We were Baptists and disapproved of that sort of thing! I was told, quite rightly, to stop being an insufferable little know-all and make myself useful.

I didn't have to watch the show anyway. I stood in the wings and handed out a flag, a gun, a parasol, or a feathered fan. Because of my good memory I was tasked with noticing the absence of a hat, a cane, spectacles or a deck of cards in a pocket, and I polished the Mounties' boots. It was over too soon. I felt at home among the greasepaint and stale tobacco smoke. I went to the Lido for a fix.

Chuck and Billy were back and told me I'd grown. 'Hmm' said Chuck 'Getting to be a big girl, but still looking like Huckleberry Finn.'

They took to rearranging my hair and pulling my socks up when they sagged. I said nothing about the bra. I'd found a way round that.

In the bottom of our knicker-drawer I'd found an old roll-on girdle of Mummy's and kept it in my satchel. At school I pulled it on to flatten my chest and stop my tunic bulging. It was hot and sometimes itchy, but better than the bumps.

### *The Cecil Hotel*

Mr Paye's house is the last address on my ID card as they went out of use that year. It had atmosphere, and aspidistras in fancy pots. It had bamboo side-tables and the world's biggest wardrobe with a centre section of drawers, and a cupboard with sliding glass shelves for laying out lace.

Arthur Road was very different. Although our room was modest, the Cecil Hotel was grand and Victorian, with a basement and four floors. It had thirteen bedrooms and a ballroom with a sprung floor. There was stained glass and fancy pillars at the front with a little sun-room above. The door was ever open. I came and went as I pleased.

Our bedsit was thirteen by fourteen feet at the very top where the last stairs emerged onto staff quarters. The occupants below seemed to be American airmen. I rarely saw them, though I sometimes heard the sound of Glen Miller drifting up in the evening. We lived in that room for two years with everything we had. It was simple and undemanding. I didn't mind. I'd stopped thinking of anywhere as home.

I saw less of Mandy and Terry after our move, though I sometimes played for a while before I walked home from school. The route took me under a railway bridge and I discovered The Dykes, wide drainage ditches beside the line, like clear streams with tiny fish and insects.

Mummy bought me the I-spy Pond-life book and we spent hours with nets and jam-jars catching stickle-backs and cadis-fly larvae. We took home whirligig beetles and watched them carry air-bubbles to breath underwater. There were pond-skaters and water-boatmen, and it felt like the Birmingham days when I was three and we had butterflies hatching in a sweetie jar; and Mummy was a magical person who knew everything and taught me to read and write and sing and dance and do sums.

My mother also bought a twelve foot oak dinghy and called it “Cynara”.

‘I am faithful unto thee, Cynara, after my fashion.’ she said, which seemed to have some cryptic significance. She decorated a swim-cap with white daisies and lay sometimes in her swimsuit, just offshore, pretending to read. Swimmers, mostly male, bobbed up around her making conversation.

I took to haunting the beach again and Mamma at the cafe sent Andros to bring me in. ‘Iss dangerous now you gettin' bigger,’ she said, ‘There's funny men out there.’ It didn't deter me. What else was there to do?

Now the thing that causes bosoms has other effects. The world took on a new intensity. Tears brimmed at little things; a tiny crab, a cloud, the sound of the funfair, and I noticed that Andros was beautiful. I liked his short white waiter's jacket, his black hair and nice teeth. I watched him all the time. I was not yet ten. I had no romantic thoughts at all, but I did want him to notice me. Sometimes I ran past him very fast in the street as if I had somewhere important to go, and hoped he was impressed. Now in old age I realise he was my first crush. I hope he has been happy.

Meanwhile, Mummy was preparing a cruelty divorce case against Daddy and regaled me with the terrible things he had done. I knew otherwise. I was there. A jug dropped in the kitchen became one thrown at her head. Installing a new washing-line became a whipping.

‘You remember, don't you dear?’ she said.

Oh yes. I remembered, but it wasn't worth arguing. This was her Gospel Truth, and wrath was called down upon unbelievers. Anyway, she said, she wouldn't need a divorce. Fate would intervene. It was in her tealeaves. She read them every day.

Bunny Baron was to be the instrument of her salvation. He was a comedian, and like all clowns, she said, he hid a tragic heart. His love for her would be his undoing. I was afraid for him, and for Daddy too. What if she was right?

# *Twenty*

There were at least four cinemas in Margate, Dreamland being the biggest. The newest films were shown there, and older ones at the others. We saw Disney's "Alice in Wonderland", Peter Ustinov in "Quo Vadis", and Mario Lanza in "The Great Caruso". We saw something most weeks and I was soon off to the library to check out the background.

## *Music and motley*

Before the BBC Light Programme was split into Radios 1 and 2, music request programmes had a mix of material covering comedy, classics, musicals, and popular songs, everything from "The Laughing Policeman" to Grand Opera.

The popular arias were from "Madame Butterfly", "Turandot", "Tosca", and there was 'Vesti la Giubba' from "I Pagliacci". I had heard them all my life, and I knew that the last was sung by a broken-hearted clown, who must paint his face and smile for his audience. I knew no more of the story.

The film of "I Pagliacci" turned up in one of the smaller cinemas and Mummy gave me her take on the story. Pagliacco was a sad clown, like Bunny Baron, she said, because another man had claimed his lady, and when he came for her Pagliacco would kill him, just as she knew Bunny would kill Daddy one day. She was so certain and so vehement that I dreaded seeing the film.

It was in black and white, and in Italian. The music and the singing had me entranced, but I couldn't make head or tail of the story. I only connected at the end as the lover struggled towards the stage and I knew what was to come.

For "Vesti la Giubba" I did not see Bunny Baron. I saw my father trying to make a joke of Mummy leaving him, breaking down at breakfast, then putting on his coat and going off to teach boys to play football. If anyone was a sad clown, it was he.

Could you read an opera like a book? Would it help me understand the plot?

I must have seemed a strange little girl, but the librarians were used to me and rustled up a libretto in a big battered book. I spent hours there. I read the English words and used a dictionary for the Italian ones, which were more informative. I got the gist.

So it seemed grown-up life was about passion ... and putting on a smile ... until the point where desperation broke out of its own accord. I found that very frightening, but one thing was certain. Opera had me hooked.

### *Odd odes.*

This was our last term in Form 3A, at Salmestone. A serious note crept in. We would move up to 4A in the autumn to study for the 11+ exam. 'Miss' made our lessons more formal, and expected our full attention.

There was still time for fun though. My friend Malcolm was, like me, into words and rhymes and reading. Together we wrote an 'odd ode' in the style of Cyril Fletcher, about Tom O'Tool, "who didn't want to go to school" and swallowed things to keep himself at home with tummy-ache.

'Miss' was impressed and suggested we do it as a shadow-play for the whole school. It was a riot and we did it in the main hall behind big white sheets backlit with old headlamps. Everyone had a job, cutting out shapes, acting, reading aloud.

A surgeon finally opened Tom up with a giant pair of scissors ...

*"And from Tom's tum he did extract*
*A string of sausages, intact,*
*A broken boot, a burst balloon*
*A whistle and an ice-cream spoon"*

I wish I could remember it all.

It was a special summer. Next year there would be goodbyes, but this year we were big enough to do new things, like scrubbing elephants for Chipperfield's Circus, or hosing down the sea lions. There were no health and safety concerns and the circus didn't mind if you made yourself useful.

I loved the elephants, and being around horses for the first time since Birmingham. Standing with my cheek against warm sides, I felt acceptable and safe. I wanted to ask the clowns about sadness, but I couldn't recognise them out of costume.

### *On and off the rails.*

In early July I was ten and I spent the summer holidays, with boobs strapped well down, making the most of being a child while I could.

The school summer holiday was six weeks long but I'm still amazed how much we packed into it that year. Big Chief I-Spy came to judge a competition. I made a collection of seaweeds. Dried and sellotaped to paper I took them to the library and labeled them in Latin. I added shells and a small tin of live specimens and won a little tepee. Mummy told people she was proud of me, and became quite companionable for a while.

Southern Railways ran a scheme called Holiday Runabout Tickets that allowed travel anywhere on the network for a week. We took the I-Spy books on birds, and flowers, and country crafts, and explored the tangle of lines that covered Kent.

Some branches led only to halts used for moving fruit and hops. Forests of apples, pears, plums and cherries stretched away from the tracks. Hop-bines towered above us. Birds sang everywhere. We walked through tiny villages and saw blacksmiths at work, and even a wheelwright; a real coup for my I-Spy book.

We covered the coast too, Roman remains, wrecks, gun emplacements, and we sat under a staging on Whitstable beach with a pic-nic salt-pot, eating fresh English tomatoes from a brown paper bag, and Mummy told me it had once been so cold that the sea had frozen there.

For a day, or an hour, she was my friend.

### *Identification.*

It was on the way home one afternoon that we met Lofty. The only other person in our compartment left for the loo. A stranger came and took his bag from the rack. Mummy whipped out her sketch-book, drew him from memory, and reported it at Margate station. We waited in the office. In walked the 'culprit', Lofty, 'a kind of policeman' Mummy said. I've no idea what it was all about but Mummy and Lofty were friends for a while, until I fell off a swing and spoiled everything.

My mother took to sketching people in the Cypriot café. She always gave them the result but used a hard pencil and carbon so she had a copy. Lofty admired her drawing skills. He was more into photographs, though I never saw him with a camera. We used our Runabout tickets to meet him in parks or station buffets in Gillingham, Rochester, or Faversham.

I don't remember Lofty speaking to me. I was invisible. He was not. He was six foot four, with a nose bent sideways, but handsome for all that. A one-time boxer, Mummy said. He wore a grey DB mac with a belt and a tie with navy/silver diagonal stripes, possibly military, but then most men had been in the forces and wore their ties with pride.

One afternoon we picnicked in the park at Faversham. Afterwards Lofty showed Mummy his photographs while she showed him her sketches and I played on the swings. I had grown self-conscious. I hunched my shoulders to hide my new boobs, and worried when the wind blew my skirt. There was no more tucking it into my knickers for handstands against the wall.

I gripped the chains of the swing, seeing how high I could go. My skirt flew up. I let go with one hand and held it down. On the next forward swing the other side of the skirt flew up and instinctively I let go with the other hand and at the highest point I slid backwards off the seat and dropped on my head.

Lofty disappeared. An ambulance came and took me to A&E. I was concussed and couldn't see. There was only Mummy's voice saying I'd spoiled everything and we could never see Lofty again.

We saw him once, briefly in a station waiting-room where Mummy handed him all her sketches and he hurried away. It was all my fault, Mummy said, for having a fit. I explained about the skirt.

Mummy said 'Nonsense!' I'd had a black-out, a seizure. 'It's epilepsy!' she said, 'I know about these things.'

### *Epilepsy 101.*

Epileptics, my mother said, had fits at precise intervals and she needed to discover mine. Twenty-four hours after I fell off the swing she sat me on a chair and watched me closely. Nothing happened.

'They must be weekly.' she said, but nothing happened after a week either.

We were in Clacton by then, to do Granny's home perm and collect the annual knitting. Mummy regaled her with the tale of my fit.

'Grand Mal,' she intoned dramatically, 'I *said* it was only a matter of time.' She predicted a fit for the 25th of every month. 'You will need to be confined on those days.'

I said that wasn't regular because months didn't have the same number of days.

'That is by the by,' said Mummy, 'We don't want you causing inconvenience and distress to others.'

Granny said she was talking through her hat, but Mummy silenced her with a threat.

'And before we go home,' she said, 'I must see that Daniel is removed from Eric's care. Whatever were they thinking?'

Daniel's term must have started sooner than ours. I learned years later that Mummy tried to drag him into a taxi on his way out of school, intent on delivering him to a children's home elsewhere. As ever, there was no comeback. It was another of Win's 'funny ideas'. A veil was drawn and life moved on.

### *Three compadres*

My mother was in a foul mood for our first few days back in Margate, and spent much time at the Lido where "Sunshine & Smiles" was nearing the end of its second season. As her temper improved I morphed in her mind from doomed mad-girl to budding genius, and she forbade me to associate any more with Mandy and Terry. They were common, she said. I would be going to grammar school next year. They would not.

We met secretly under the pier. We pooled pocket-money and had photos taken, but the little girls of April were no more. Terry, between us, looked slightly alarmed, while Mandy and I showed hints of the women we would become. We were growing fast. By the end of the year the little girls would be gone.

Of course there was no guarantee that *any* of us would get to grammar school, as I soon found out. Mr Walker summoned me the first week of term and explained.

We were part of a baby-boom. At Salmestone, Class 4 had A, B, and C streams with up to forty pupils in each. Other Kent schools had similar numbers. The county delivered the 11+ in two stages. Pass the first and you could sit the second.

Of a hundred or so pupils at Salmestone there would be five Grammar School places for boys and three for girls.

'Gosh!' I said 'That's not fair! There are more clever people than that! It's like a lucky-dip!'

Mr Walker said 'It's up to you then, isn't it? Change the world. Make it fairer. But first you must pass the exam.'

Until now I'd had extra access to Mr Walker, sharing my extra-curricular discoveries from the library. Now, he said, this must stop. There could be no whiff of favouritism in this final year. I understood.

'I want you to do something for me, Elizabeth. I want you to learn only from the page your teacher gives you. Don't read further on, and don't seek extra information elsewhere. The questions in the exams will *only* be about class-work. If you write anything else you will lose marks."

'Can't I go to the library then?'

'Of course you can, but steer clear of the school subjects. Read some fiction. Write some more funny rhymes. And don't worry about the exams. Good luck.'

### *Inspiration*

Oddly enough I felt good. I felt I'd been entrusted with something, a challenge, a mission. And there was no trouble concentrating in class because this year we had Mr Stafford; and Mr Stafford was special.

To look at, there was nothing remarkable about Mr Stafford. He was an average Dad-looking chap, fortyish, lived in Ramsgate and cycled to Margate every morning. It was his teaching style that set him apart. I saw nothing like it before or since, and no one since my father had gripped or inspired me, or stretched my world the way he did.

This being a primary school, Mr Stafford took us for all subjects, and although there was a rough timetable, he blended one subject into another so that a change of period was sometimes just a change of focus. I wasn't bored for a minute.

That autumn term Mr Stafford began with Ordinance Survey Maps. We learned all the symbols; roads and forests and marshes, windmills, castles and historic ruins. The maps led to maths, where we used contours to raise the outlines of hills, or plot routes across country.

The marks for burial mounds brought us into history and we learned about woad, (a bit of science and nature study there), and Julius Caesar (54BC). We had King Alfred, and Wessex, King Canute, Hengist and Horsa, Hereward the Wake, the Conquest, and then the ordinary people, serfs and villeins and Lords of the Manors.

Towards the end of term we did crop rotation, strip culture, three-field systems in mediaeval villages and, just in time for Christmas, The Black Death and leprosy. We did the latter in the Scripture period, which moved subtly from healing miracles to modern medicine, and we first heard of Dr Schweitzer. 'Next term,' said Mr Stafford, 'We're going to explore Africa.' I could hardly wait.

### *It's who you know ...*

Mummy took me to a film called "Mandy" about a deaf child being taught to speak. It starred Mandy Miller and Mummy's plans for me changed again. I was to be a famous child actress.

'But what about my fits?'

'We have passed the 25th of September now so you obviously only have a seizure once a year.'

I was relieved, but she said 'That doesn't mean you are at all sane, Elizabeth! You are still an Innes.'

I cried. Mummy was always tender once I cried. 'Don't worry, darling.' she said 'I'll look after you.'

'And Grammar School?'

'You can forget about *that*! You will go to RADA. Robert Donat will get you in.'

Sure enough, crossing London to Granny's in December, Robert came walking towards us at Victoria Station, with two other men. We crowded into a taxi and had tea somewhere posh where a man played a grand piano and there were real meringues. They talked and laughed, while I indulged my new interest in the beauty of the adult male.

Robert's eyes were mesmerising, dark and liquid, but his mouth was unattractive and his teeth too small. No matter, I was more fascinated by Stewart Granger. Just as handsome as he was on screen. I couldn't take my eyes off him, which is probably why I always imagined the third man might have been Leo Genn. It wasn't. In 1996 I was reunited with my autograph book. It was Andre Morel.

We visited Robert once after that. He had an Oscar he used to keep the bathroom door shut. Mummy went on at length about my talents, but when she went to the loo Robert said, 'and what do *you* want to do?'

'I want to be a scientist. You know. Atoms and things.'

'Do you now?' he said, raising an eyebrow.

'Yes. Seriously.' The eyebrow came down.

'Well, if you change your mind, remember in this business it's not what you know but *who* you know that matters.'

Robert died in 1958, before I could take him up on that.

### *Blessings and curses.*

Christmas was a nightmare despite Granny's attempts at cheerfulness. Mummy held forth about Daddy, and how she would get Daniel removed. The man was a pervert, she said. Granny said his expectations had been quite normal. I wondered what that meant.

'You *would* say that!' mummy squeaked 'You're all as bad as he is and God will curse you to hell!' She stuck the poker in the fire, and Granny hurried me off to help with dinner.

When we returned, Mummy was drawing patterns in the air with the glowing poker. With the Bible in her other hand, she called upon God to deny Daddy warmth, shelter and food and to curse anyone who provided them. Then she switched her face to 'calm', put the Bible away and laid the table.

I was feeling edgy and this didn't help. Keeping calm always served me best, but it was getting harder. Sometimes I snapped at Mummy and got a slap. If I lost my temper it would prove the Innes madness, but I didn't know how long I could hold on. I had dreadful cramps in my stomach. Maybe God was punishing me.

On New Year's Eve Granny went to a Church meeting after tea and as I undressed, God's anger fell upon me. I was bleeding! Bleeding to death! I was distraught.

'I'm sorry, Mummy! I'm sorry for my bad thoughts.'

My mother took one look and shook me hard. She stood me on the kitchen table and examined me. She said I'd been touching myself. She put an elastic belt and pad on me, said I was a freak of nature, and born immoral and sent me to bed where I cried myself to sleep.

A shaft of light from the doorway. The silhouette of Granny's hat.

'It's only me,' she whispered, 'Can I come in?'

She brought cocoa and a hot-water bottle for my sore tum.

'My goodness, what's this?' she said, grinning. And she sat and explained, and rubbed the small of my back, sitting there in her pinny, with her hat still on her head.

'Never mind the hat,' she said, 'It's quite safe where it is.' and she kissed me goodnight.

# *Twenty-one*

Back in 1953 America swore in a new president, and fewer people tuned in to watch Eisenhower than the previous night's figure for "I Love Lucy". I was only ten but talk in the Cypriot Cafe sparked my interest. Pappa thought Ike got in on his war record, and Adlai Stevenson should have got the job.

Opinion was divided among the men of USAAF Manston, smoking their Philip Morris over tea, and beans on toast.

Pappa said, 'You can't vote for Ike just cos he's in the military.'

Some nodded.

'He wants to nukilate the Koreans. One day somebody does it back.' He waved his hands helplessly.

There was no sign of Mummy, so I just waited and listened, and wrote in my notebook.

'We will always have bigger ones.' somebody said.

Pappa said something vehement in Greek. 'So you make bigger, bigger bomps till you make one that kill the whole world. Then what you do? ... UH?'

'Cain't talk about bombs, pal. The deal goes with the uniform.'

'Then I tell you!' said Pappa undeterred, 'You do nothing. Coz there be no you to do it ... No you ... No me ... No nobody.'

That was scary. I seriously wished the other man had won the election. I would look him up in the library. 'How do you spell Adlai Stevenson?' I said.

The librarians were used to me. British seaweeds, wheelwrights, fossils, Operatic libretti, they fulfilled my every desire. This was a new one.

'I want to know about Adlai Stevenson.' I said 'Is he in the Brittanica?'

They did better than that and brought me copies of Time magazine, and a book with speeches. I didn't understand half of it, but I wanted to so very much. The librarian said I might make a writer, as I was interested in so much ... or maybe a journalist.

A journalist. I hadn't thought of that. I wandered up to the local paper and asked what I had to do. The editor indulged me. The first thing was to learn shorthand, and to practice getting lots of information into as few words as possible. Would I like him to set me a practice piece and he'd let me know if I had promise. Yes please!

'Something on hats then.'

'Hats?'

'Or shoes or dresses. You could see what's new in the window at Bobbies.'

'I don't want to write about clothes. I could write about Adlai Stevenson.'

The editor said 'Oh dear' in the same tone my teachers did sometimes.

He said, 'I'd leave politics to us chaps if I were you. You needn't bother your ...'

*('... pretty little head' I could hear it coming.)*

I thanked him for seeing me and shook his hand solemnly. He looked surprised.

'I'm sorry,' I said, 'I don't think I can help you.' He was about to say that to me I knew, so I said it first.

I liked the way Stevenson used words. 'Pompous phrases marching across the landscape in search of an idea.' he said of Ike's administration. I made a note of it and years later found the same quotation scribbled in my father's notebook.

Mr Walker wanted to speak to me about the 11+ exam, and get my reassurance that I was not reading extra stuff in the library, but concentrating on the lessons. I promised I was only reading about Eisenhower and Stevenson at the moment and he said 'Oh dear.' in the way I'd come to expect.

Then he said, 'Put your hands flat on my desk.' I complied. He picked them up and looked at my nails, bitten to the quick, and as a private agreement offered me sixpence for every nail I could grow by the time I left that summer. ‘That's half a crown a handful.’ he said.

I failed. I cost him nothing, and bit my nails for another forty-seven years.

### *'Gainst wind and tide.*

One Saturday afternoon at the end of the month I was waiting for a bus, not at the bus-stop, but hanging for dear life to the sea-front railings, while the wind thrashed at my body and tried to snatch my satchel. The grey sea heaved and sucked. There was no one else about but for the bus across the street, waiting to take me up the Northdown Road. But I daren’t let go of the railings.

Suddenly, the driver and conductor dashed across the road, seized me by the arms and raced me back to the bus. It rocked as the wind hit the upper deck and we left at once.

‘Lord! You gev us a fright,’ the conductor said, ‘Stay away from the railings, ducky. Thought you was gettin' sucked out to sea.’

I was the only passenger, wet with sea-spray, shivering. My socks squelched in my shoes. I'd be glad to get home.

It was more sheltered in Arthur Rd, and even high in our bedsit at The Cecil Hotel, the wind made little noise. Mummy was out. I wasn't allowed to sit in her chair, or lie on the bed in case I creased it, so I sat on the floor and waited. I couldn't light the fire. Mummy had the sixpences for the gas meter and only put one in when she was home. I wondered if I'd be in trouble for getting wet.

Mummy came in, as wet as I was, laughing and braced by the weather. Water dripped from her sopping headscarf. She put *two* sixpences in the meter and made sardines on toast, and cocoa. We huddled side by side before the little fire, steaming gently, and listening to the news. There was a storm, they said. As if we needed telling.

Bed felt warm and luxurious, if a little clammy from the moisture in the air, but my mac was nearly dry by morning, and I couldn't wait to get out. In the street I met a girl who said her name was Hilary. There were floods in town and we should go and have a look. We were quite unprepared for what we found.

As Hilary and I came down the hill into Duke Square we found it flooded, and the town in chaos. My mother's dinghy Cynara had been thrown over the harbour wall, and a street's length inland. Miraculously undamaged, she was moored to a bus-stop with two policemen aboard, rescuing people from the alms-houses. Half a dozen fire-hoses pumped water back towards the shore. We picked our way among them down the narrow street.

The sea-front was devastated and roped off. We couldn't see far, but we could see enough. Much of the railing was gone, the lamp-stands twisted by some giant hand. There were holes feet deep in the tarmac, exposing pipes and wires, and there were spars, planks and broken boats everywhere. The pier was almost stripped.

The wind had lessened but the sea still raged. At the end of the stone jetty giant waves crashed against the lighthouse. It looked slightly off the vertical. Perhaps it was my eyes.

As we watched, it fell. The jetty collapsed, undermined by the storm, and the lighthouse sank, almost regally at first. It dropped straight down then broke in three. The lantern toppled into the sea, the tower fell, and the base disappeared with the crumbling harbour wall.

We'd seen enough. We walked back up the Northdown Road and tried to reach the Lido. It was a wreck. From the cliff-top we could see hunks of concrete torn from the sides of the swimming pool and thrown up onto the parade. The kiosks and cafes were torn apart and all the beach, back to the harbour was strewn with timber from the devastated pier and its buildings. The theatre looked OK, but we couldn't get near enough to see.

It was deeply depressing. “Sunshine & Smiles” was due back in spring ... and what about the Coronation? How could it all be mended?

It was Sunday so everything was shut. There was nothing to do but go home and listen to the Billy Cotton Band Show with Mummy ... and the One o'clock News.

### *... and elsewhere.*

We listened to the news next morning. A thousand miles of British coast was damaged. Hundreds of people had drowned on land, and hundreds more at sea on trawlers and a ferry. Yet we were lucky. In Holland the sea- walls had broken and maybe two thousand people were dead. It was more than I could bear. I chose to walk to school so that I could cry on the way.

In assembly we said prayers for people in the Netherlands and sang "For those in peril on the sea." with such passion that I still choke up when I hear it.

I thought about the words. Whatever was God *thinking*? He was supposed to "bind the restless wave" wasn't he? And if he bade the mighty oceans to keep "their own appointed limits" they obviously weren't listening. I wished it was OK to ask questions about God, but it wasn't.

We heard from Granny in Clacton. She was fine and well away from the sea. Jaywick, though, had been trashed and people had died. Mummy's Lewisham cousins were also fine but the storm-surge had run up the Thames into the East End, backed up the drains and washed half London's sewage into Canning Town. The river was a mess.

In Margate I combed the streets and cliff-tops with my friends, rescuing crabs, shrimps and shellfish and returning them to the sea. It's surprising how much you can do when everyone mucks in. Surprising too, how quickly the timber disappeared from the beaches and how many rough new sheds appeared on the allotments, complete with barnacles.

The Victorian railings were found in sections and carted off for repair and pot-holes quickly filled. Glaziers worked overtime and painters stood ready for better weather. We had suffered far less than others and were thankful.

The countryside took longer to recover. Margate is in the county of Kent, the bottom right-hand corner of Britain. Its northern coast is part of the Thames estuary, and where the estuary meets the sea there is a nose, a bump, called the North Foreland, an area of chalk cliffs, golden beaches and the seaside towns of Margate, Ramsgate and Broadstairs.

The area between, built up now, was cornfields and orchards then, and the Manston Air Base. Idyllic post-war Britain.

The Foreland is part of Thanet, once an island off the Kent coast, but joined to the mainland by centuries of silt. Protected by sea-walls the old channel evolved into rich farmland under tender human care. Now Thanet was an island again. The wall had breached. The railway line along its crest hung in midair. Salt water flooded the low-lying farms. Mr Stafford gave us a lesson on soils, their organisms and structure, and what might grow where it was salty. Beetroot he thought. He had an allotment. He knew these things.

### *Another tongue.*

Sweets came off ration. Not that we bought more than usual. It was a cash flow problem. Most sweets were sold loose from big glass jars and cost sixpence a quarter (125gm) Cough sweets were only thruppence a quarter and never rationed so we'd always bought them anyway.

There were two kinds, cherry menthol and licorice. They stained our tongues and for playground games we divided into the Red-Tongue and Black-tongue tribes beginning our day by walking round sticking our tongues out at each other as a means of identification. You didn't have to be the same colour every day, so there were always surprises. Kids with money to burn sometimes brought pear-drops or sherbet lemons but that just labeled them as show-offs.

Class 4A had lots of questions for Mr Stafford about the floods and why they'd happened, but he said we would do England in the summer, but this term we were doing Africa. As ever he melded subjects together. He started with Geography, and History, drawing an outline of Africa on the board with just the major rivers.

So we learned about Mungo Park; Burton, Speke and Grant; Livingstone and Stanley. We tramped up the Niger, the Nile, the Zambezi, the Limpopo and Congo Rivers, encountering wild animals, strange foods and gruesome diseases. One of these was leprosy, which tied in with Scripture lessons, and Science. We heard about Dr

Schweitzer's leper colony at Lamborene and were amazed when Mr Stafford played us a record in the music period of Schweitzer playing the organ. He said we didn't have to be good at only one thing, and everybody was good at something.

Coming in to a maths lesson one day we found a cartoon drawn on the board. A man with an elephant on each outstretched arm and another balanced on his head. Beside it was written the average weight of an elephant, the average skin area of a six foot male in inches, and the average air-pressure per square inch at sea-level. So what was the total weight of the air on this man ... in elephants; and why didn't that question make sense? The solution strayed into meteorology, osmosis, and vacuums. It was such fun that I've never forgotten. I wish I knew more about Mr Stafford. He was an inspiration.

# *Twenty-two*

My mother said it was immoral to read newspapers on Sundays, but I knew she bought the News of the World and kept it under her pillow. I read it when she was out. We lived in a single room, for goodness sake! What did she expect?

The News of the World was a scurrilous rag at best, but its current obsessions were Craig and Christie. Craig had shot a policeman but only his friend Bentley had been hanged. There were letters and arguments. We talked about it in the playground.

Christie, however, was someone children should not know about. Parents had been hiding papers throughout the trial, but we knew. Now Christie was hanged, but had let Evans go to the gallows wrongly convicted. Some of my friends had nightmares. Grown-ups could make mistakes. Innocent people could die.

Mummy said I would hang eventually. I would kill. It was in my blood. I wouldn't be able to help myself. She told me why the knot was the shape it was, and how the length of the rope must be right for your weight. I didn't respond. I refused to cry or plead. She read my tealeaves.

'If you get the right hangman it will be quick,' she said, softly reassuring. 'or perhaps you'll fall under a train.'

She told me a tale of a woman who had magic ballet slippers that wouldn't let her stop dancing so she leapt under a train to end their power. We went to see Moira Shearer in "The Red Shoes" I knew how it would end, but just as she leapt Mummy thrust her arm across my eyes.

'Why did you DO that?' I demanded, hurrying after her down the street.

'Because I want you to *imagine*.' she said.

'But I don't want to die under a train, Mummy.'

'It will be better than hanging.' she said and hurried off.

I slipped down a side street and went for a walk. I wanted to please her. I wanted her to like me. Did I have to die to make it happen? But I wouldn't know, would I, because I'd be dead. And anyway I wanted to grow up ... to be older than ten ... to have a home and babies. But what if I killed one of them? I would hang just as she said. My thoughts went round and round. I sat in a bus shelter and didn't go home for tea.

### *The annual song and dance.*

The room we lived in was about fifteen feet square, most of it taken up by a double-bed. Everything we had was in there and every inch of wall had furniture against it.

My side of the bed had a dining chair for my clothes, Mummy's bureau, and down the side wall, a sink and draining-board, treadle sewing-machine and a narrow table. On Mummy's side another chair and the door, with a dressing-chest, and folding table along the wall. We lived in the six foot space between the foot of the bed and the chimney breast where there was a small gas fire. Mummy had an armchair. I sat on the floor.

In the alcove left of the fire was a wardrobe with full length mirror and to the right a two-ring gas stove with a small oven. The rings were currently occupied by pans of wax. We were making flowers.

Margate Operatic Society was doing "Magyar Melody" and Mummy was props and wardrobe as before. In one big dance scene the girls danced with hoops and ropes festooned with flowers and wheat. Mummy bought a How-to Book and a lot of crepe paper and wire.

For weeks we snipped and rolled and shaped. I bound miles of green paper onto wires and our drab room became a riot of cornflowers, poppies and white daisies. The poppies were waxed to keep their petals stiff, and all were pinned in bunches round the picture rail. Eventually we loaded them into a taxi and took them to the Hippodrome. We had blisters on our fingers, but it was worth it for the stunning sight on stage.

The costumes arrived and there were boots again; all for me to polish daily. Last year it was Canadian Mounties, now it was dancing boots for Csárdás. Maybe next year they'd do something barefoot! I didn't mind really. I just loved being part of it and watching Mummy being an expert ... and being happy. She was kind when she was happy.

Interesting things were happening at school. We had a visit from a writer. Anthony Buckeridge lived in Ramsgate and was author of the Jennings novels, famously dramatised for the BBC. Set in a boys' prep school they were full of 'jolly japes' and 'wizard wheezes' designed to gain advantage over adults and avoid punishment. Spiffing stuff, old bean!

Buckeridge gave his talk in the main hall, to all the third and fourth forms. Being a girl I wasn't that interested in Jennings and his friend Darbishire, but what Buckeridge did was take us through the whole process of producing a book.

He covered writing, editing, and proof-reading, printing, publication, publicity, launches, and signings. He showed us galley-proofs, and manuscripts with scribbles everywhere. He showed us the special marks an author makes to indicate changes.

He said it was important to get get on with your next book right away while the lights were still on in your mind, and he waved a little book at us, Strunk and White's "Elements of Style" and said we should remember it's name. I did, though it was fifty years before I bought my copy.

### *Matters of life and death.*

We went to Clacton at Easter. We stayed away from the seafront. I didn't want to see the storm-damage.

It was a treat to have a bed to myself upstairs, to turn out the light and get some sleep. My mother only slept four hours a night and always woke at four-thirty or five and sat up beside me writing long letters to “authorities”, periodicals and her solicitor, concerning the perceived wrong-doing of others, especially my father. She used carbons and spread an old towel on her lap to keep ink from the sheets.

In summer I often slept under the pier after school with my head on my satchel, but the weather was cold now and there were days I was so tired I felt nauseous.

I had questions for Granny, but it was hard to get her on her own. Mummy followed us around and there was no chance of reassurance or hugs. I wrote my questions down and tried to pass one to her each bedtime, but she found no time to answer.

Since Mummy's remarks about hanging I'd thought a lot about death ... or at least about killing. If "Thou shalt not kill" applied to everyone, was the hangman guilty of killing the condemned murderer, or was it the judge who sentenced him? And what about all the soldiers who kill and the pilots who drop the bombs? Would God understand when they said they were ordered to do it, or was everyone going to hell?

According to Mummy they were, except for God's sinless elect. Granny said 'Hrumph!' and the loose bit under her chin wobbled.

### *The balance of the mind*

Mummy was super-busy that holiday. Granny had her home perm and we let down the hems of my summer frocks. But the highlight was designing my costume for the Margate Coronation Carnival.

Queen Elizabeth the First: They pored over diagrams of farthingales and Medici collars. They experimented on dolls using muslin and wire. They drew more diagrams. They measured me minutely, which I didn't mind and fiddled with my hair, which I did.

Time was running out. I needed a second opinion on my road to the gallows. I'd just have to speak out in front of Mummy. A mealtime seemed best but they were arguing about my school cardigans for autumn. Granny said she wouldn't know what colour until we knew if I'd passed 11+.

'Of course she'll pass,' said Mummy, 'She'll go to the Grammar School in Ramsgate.' It was now or never ...

'It doesn't matter anyway if I'm going to die,' I said, 'Mummy says I'll hang if I don't kill myself first; under a train like in "The Red Shoes."'

Granny said not to be silly but Mummy squeezed my hand and said 'You don't have to, Elizabeth. There are lots of other ways to do it.'

Granny said 'WIN! What have you been saying?'

Mummy didn't answer.

Granny said, 'Suicide is against the law, Elizabeth. It's murder just as sure as if you'd killed someone else.'

'But they can't punish you if you're dead, Granny.'

'But they can punish your family. They say the balance of your mind was disturbed, and your will is useless because you weren't sane when you made it.'

'She hasn't anything to leave.' said Mummy. Granny glared at her.

Granny went on, '... and if you try and fail you are had up for a crime.'

'Then she'd better make a good job of it!'

'Win!! Please! That is ENOUGH!'

Mummy was looking at me the way she used to look at Daddy. I was trying not to cry. Did she hate me as much as that? Of course not. Mummies loved their babies. God made it that way. Everybody said so.

Granny tried to change the subject but it was too late. I burst out, 'I want to grow up. I want to have babies and a nice house.'

Mummy said it wouldn't be possible because of the Innes blood and anyway I might not really be a woman.

'Of course I'm a woman! I've got BOSOMS!'

'Some people have both,' said Mummy, 'They're called hermaphrodites. We'll have to keep an eye on you.'

I wanted to throw my dinner at her, but it was one of Granny's nice plates, and anyway, Mummy would just say it proved I was violent. I fled the room and Granny ran after me.

'Leave her alone,' Mummy called, 'she just wants attention.'

### *Old Lace*

We visited Auntie Mary next door. She was getting deafer and losing her sight but always good for a tale. She was upset about the recent death of Queen Mary, and sad that the Duke of Windsor was still an exile. She had nursed him and his siblings through chicken-pox long ago and was deeply hurt by his abdication, though she expected it was for the best.

Among the cast-off items salvaged from Osborne House were lace samples supplied for the Queen's Diamond Jubilee dresses. There were edgings and inserts of fronds and pomegranates, some as wide as six inches, in black, silver or gold with real metal thread woven in. Each was framed on pale blue card with scribbled notes. As Mummy finished my Carnival costume I was horrified to find that she had removed the gold samples from their cards and used them down the front of my dress.

'She won't miss them.' said Mummy, as she used another piece in a fan. That wasn't the point. They should have stayed in their mounts, as they were when Queen Victoria handled them. It was an act of wanton vandalism that still makes me shudder. Naturally, I dared not complain.

### *Rule Brittania!*

As the Summer term began Britain went into patriotic overdrive. There were eight weeks to the Coronation. Painters and sign-writers were on ladders all along the parade refurbishing the shop-fronts. And Salmestone School had whole-school music sessions focused on songs about the Thames.

"From the Cotswolds, from the Chilterns, From your fountains and your springs. Flow down, O London River, To the seagulls' silver wings." we sang; and Mr Stafford showed us the Cotswolds on a map and we traced the Thames across England to the sea. He told us a history of England from Caesar through Boadicea to Alfred and on to the Norman conquest.

There were outings to Roman remains at Reculver and Richborough. Mr Stafford told us about St Augustine's arrival in Kent, drew a plan of a monastery and told us it's daily routine. We went to Minster on the bus and walked on ground where Augustine trod before he went to Canterbury. Then he told us about the Venerable Bede.

I liked Bede. He spoke Old English as well as Latin ... and he knew how to die. He translated the Gospel of St John, we were told, and when he'd dictated the last line he just "turned his face to the wall" and died. So with a bit of cooperation from God, you could go when you chose. That was a relief!

Mr Stafford played us his own favourite Thames song. History, he told us, was like a river, it flowed out of the past and on into the future, always changing, but still the same river, like "Old Father Thames". I went to the library and copied the words. I wished I could be like a river, and just get on with it, following the slope of the land. Maybe I could. I'd have to think about it.

*"He never seems to worry,*
*Doesn't care for fortune's fame.*
*He never seems to hurry,*
*But he gets there just the same.*
*Kingdoms may come. Kingdoms may go.*
*Whatever the end may be.*
*Old Father Thames keeps rolling along.*
*Down to the mighty sea."*

The singer on Mr Stafford's record was Peter Dawson, a bass-baritone like my father. It sounded like Daddy giving advice. It was two years since I'd seen him. Where was he? Where was Daniel? I wanted to hear the song again. I looked on all the juke-boxes but the song wasn't there.

# *Twenty-three*

Margate was gearing up for a special summer. Everyone was upbeat. "Sunshine & Smiles" was back for a third season. At the cafe, Andros was back too. He had spent the winter in Cyprus but returned with a big black moustache. I was heartbroken. My beautiful Andros was gone. He was taller. He was a grown-up. A MAN! And so ended my first crush. I don't think he ever knew.

### *Flags and farthingales.*

Decorations went up. One weekend Mummy and I went to her school in Ramsgate and wove a Union Jack over the entire ceiling of her classroom, in inch-wide strips of crepe paper. It took us two days and hundreds of thumb-tacks.

My Queen Bess costume was almost ready. It was demanding to wear, but interesting to know how Tudor women lived. The width of the farthingale required that hands remain modestly together in front of you. Pressure to one side tipped the other upwards. The high collar stopped you turning your head. The stomacher came to a sharp point at the crotch and was completely rigid so that you had to remain upright. Sitting was an art.

In the midst of all this I sat the exams. There were a lot of them. Records say that the 11+ was relatively basic, but I sat papers in History and Geography as well as a lengthy intelligence test, possibly the entrance exam for a particular school. No one explained. I turned up on time. I sat and wrote when told. I just got on with it. Like "Old Father Thames", there was absolutely no stress.

I was still worried about Heaven and Hell. I sought comfort at the library. Had they anything by Bede, I asked. They found me quotes, in Latin and English.

One said that life was short and what came before or after we could not know. Ah! So heaven and hell were just a guess. I copied it into my book. "

*"quid autem sequatur, quidue praecesserit, prorsus ignoramus."*

That was interesting. 'Ignoramus' must mean not knowing.

'If I pass my exams I shall learn Latin at Ramsgate.' I told the librarians, who said they looked forward that.

It occurred to me that I needed a special script for my diary. I started with a code from one of my comics, involving grids and dots. I added up my birthday numbers and moved the alphabet six spaces forward. In the end my script had code-shapes, letters upside down or back-to-front, along with Cyrillic, Hebrew, adapted Chinese pictographs and Egyptian hieroglyphs. I adapted a heart-shape into a letter and used Egyptian Ka for soul. It was impenetrable to others, and eventually even to me.

### *Queen and country.*

Mr Stafford brought in an outline of the Coronation Service and worked our lessons around its meaning, including the regalia.

Mummy liked this idea. She dragged her foot-powered fret-saw from under the bed and started on a model of the State Coach, along with replicas of the three main crowns.

Meanwhile Mr Stafford told us how an ancient 'king' was the head of a 'kin' or family. In Old English this was a 'cyng'. His wife was the 'cwen' which was Old English for 'woman' or in this case '*the* woman' because a coronation was a kind of wedding with his queen representing the land he promised to cherish. This was important, because if we didn't cherish it we'd starve.

A Queen alone didn't need a king. She represented the land herself and her coronation was a special and holy thing. So the Duke of Edinburgh would only be a Prince Consort. When he knelt at her feet he would swear allegiance not to her, but to the soil of Britain ... to Britannia. We were rapt. No one fidgeted.

We asked if Britannia was a Goddess, and did that annoy God? Mr Stafford said St Augustine had sorted things out with God and moved quickly on to why the earth had to be cherished. We kept him on the hook and gave him a hard time.

He had taught us well this past year, taught us to think and question. I suspect he was a bit of a rebel. So ... there was God ... and Jesus ... but all over the world there were people who gave names to ideas and called them gods. I was satisfied with that.

### *Sleepless in Thanet*

Behind the closed door of our little bedsit, my mother had reverted to gypsy mode, divining with playing cards, dice, dominoes, even apple peels. Bunny Baron was in love with her, as was Robert Donat. They simply didn't realise. She just needed the cards to confirm it.

Out in the wide world she was Miss Prim at school, and a super-luvvie at the theatre, switching roles at the click of a door and a change of gloves. Now, with a Coronation in view she was the great-niece of Queen Victoria's nurse and practically royal by association. The carnival organisers loved her.

I came in one day to find Mummy standing on her head with heels against the wardrobe. 'Put the kettle on, dear,' she mumbled through her blouse, which had dropped over her face. I made tea.

'It's called yoga, you know,' said Mummy, 'Ten minutes on your head is worth eight hours of sleep.'

She needed it. Model-making was all. She was consumed with zeal as if she couldn't stop. There were nights when I don't think she came to bed at all. I pulled the covers over me to shut out the light, the sound of the fretsaw, and the smell of glue and paint. There was sawdust everywhere. It was in the bed, it was in my socks and sometimes in my dinner.

In the end it was worth it. The golden coach with its horses was four feet long and was displayed at my school. The replica crowns hung in the sunroom over the hotel porch, the St Edward, the State Crown, and the one for the Queen mother. There were coronets for a Duke, an Earl and a Baron in cardboard, crepe paper and ping-pong balls, all full size, and visible from both ends of the street.

Another thing I learned that year was how much you could achieve even when you had to sleep, work, wash and cook in just one room. I was glad though, when I didn't have to squeeze past the fretsaw to get round the end of the bed.

Strangely, however manic and extreme it was, the models, and the flowers we made for "Magyar Melody" taught me that if you want to put on a good show you need to go above and beyond, though perhaps *not* into the stratosphere.

### *Vivat Regina!*

On Coronation Day we listened on the radio in our room. The Bakelite speaker crackled from its perch on top of the wardrobe, relayed throughout the hotel. The service went on for hours. Richard Dimbleby murmured from some high perch in the Abbey. Something arcane took place beneath a golden canopy. Then Elizabeth was crowned and Philip swore to be her "liege man of life and limb". The cheers outside were deafening. Later, when the film was shown in cinemas you had to queue to get in.

I had reservations, even then, about the concept of Empire and the arrogant enforcement of Christianity, but what moved me was that this young woman, the age of a big sister, represented the earth beneath my feet and was crowned seated on oak that spread its first roots in that earth more than a thousand years before. It moves me still.

There were fireworks on Coronation night ending with the Queen's head written in flame, and a whole ox was roast on a spit in the Dreamland Amusement Park. At the carnival I wore my farthingale and won second prize in the children's fancy dress. Then it was all over.

At school we asked Mr Stafford about the unicorn on the coat of arms and he produced tales of mythical beasts and Greek gods, Minotaurs, Gorgons and golden apples.

Optimism remained for a long time. There was much talk of good Queen Bess and Shakespeare, and England as a "precious jewel set in a silver sea." But the sea wasn't always silver, we knew. We had seen what it could do.

* * *

### *Up the social ladder.*

The exam results came in. I had passed.

Mr Stafford reorganised the class moving the 'passers' to the front. I missed Malcolm. I'd shared a desk with him all year. He made me laugh and had once written 'THIS WAY UP' on his finger and put it through a hole in his pocket and out through his fly. When he nudged me and nodded for me to look down I burst into such giggles that we both had to stand in the corridor ... for laughing that is ... we never let on why.

There were just three girls' grammar places for Salmestone Primary. I had one of them. I exchanged gossip with the other two about Ramsgate, its staff and uniform. Eventually we stood together in Mr Walker's office. We were the New Elizabethans, he said. The future was up to us. He talked about the Ramsgate curriculum, languages, sport, literature.

'Elizabeth, however, will be going to Folkestone.'

'Pardon!'

'Did your mother not tell you?'

'No, Sir. Does that mean we're moving again?' A guillotine hovered over my friendships.

Mr Walker said 'No. You will be boarding. You have a scholarship.'

Boarding school! Graphics from girls' comics flooded my mind, "Girls' Crystal", "School Friend", lacrosse sticks, weekend exeats, and midnight feasts in the dorm. I was shocked, excited, and mightily relieved that we would still live in Margate.

After that the 'passers' became classroom royalty, different and separate, as if a scythe had passed through the school and mown down all my friends.

Mandy said, 'Never mind, you can come back in the holidays and tell us what it's like.'

I asked her why she and Terry liked me. She said other people were just scared because I was clever.

'We don't mind you being clever,' she said, 'Coz you're kind.' I was going to miss them.

I worked out that there were around eighty of us in the three streams of Class 4, so that meant there was a Grammar School place for one in ten. I hung about after school and asked Mr Stafford if that was the same all over Kent. It was.

So in our school it was the eight people with the highest marks? It was. So people at other schools with more children and more places might get less marks but go to Grammar School anyway? It jolly well wasn't fair. Mr Stafford would not discuss it further.

My responses to the world about me grew intense. A mixture of hormones and growing confidence I guess. Almost everything moved me one way or another. I was scared. I wanted to be sensible and restrained and ladylike, but inside I was Little Miss Outraged of Margate, on a mission to save the world!

I could understand it being good to pass an exam. It was good to have climbed Everest, or sing like Mario Lanza, but that didn't mean the rest of us had failed, did it? So why, when you got into Grammar School, was everyone else made small and somehow dirty.

I needed to let off steam and the only way I knew was with words. But I hadn't written poetry since we left Clacton and I'd been a child then, writing about flowers and squirrels and the weather. I was too big for that now. Grown-up poetry seemed to be about flowers too, or lost loves, sea-battles and Gods. Where were the poems that *said* something? If I wanted to write like that, I must read things like that. I would ask at the library.

### *Rhyme and reason.*

Mr Stafford filled the rest of the term with interesting stuff about land reclamation, how Holland was repairing the flooded polders, what might be done about farmland around Thanet. We learned about the Outer Hebrides using seaweed to turn sand into soil. I learned a new word 'machair', the sandy grasslands beside the western seas.

Lessons became relaxed and Mr Stafford had the 'passers' improving their handwriting, (a lost cause in my case) and cheered the others with tales of opportunities for work in hotels around the coast, and factories in London. In the school hall we sang of 'England's green and pleasant land'.

Not for everyone it wasn't! I knew that. I remembered my earliest journeys to and fro between Birmingham and London. Past tall chimneys puthering out smoke that slid down their sides in cold weather or mingled with low cloud above; running out through Coventry and Rugby into green countryside and then back into smokey London and more tall chimneys, among the blitzed remains of tenements and warehouses. Is that all you got if you failed 11+?

Did poets ever speak their mind or was it just not done? I asked at the library for poets with something to say. They brought me an anthology and I found what I wanted. Charlotte Mew lamenting *"Hurt not the trees!"* And Kipling:

*'It's "Tommy this", and "Tommy that",*
*And "Chuck him out, the brute".*
*But it's "Thank you, Mr Atkins"*
*When the guns begin to shoot.'*

That's what I needed; someone with a bit of fire.

I read and read and when I felt ready I started to write my first grown-up poem. There was just one verse. Two more verses came in the next three years, the last of which got me into real hot water. It wasn't very good but it said what I wanted. It was a start.

*The factory chimneys like warders are standing*
*Their guard o'er the people who live in this town,*
*Keeping them prisoners, sentenced by others*
*Who know not of Beauty's great grace and renown.*
*And Britannia's sad eyes look down on her folk*
*As she weeps from her throne in the clouds high above*
*'What have they done to my beautiful England?*
*What have they done to the land that I love?'*
(C)1953: Elizabeth Innes. Aged 11.

# *Twenty-four*

Whoever put me in for a scholarship it certainly wasn't Mummy. She was annoyed. She said she had other plans for me but wouldn't say what. Making me a child-star? Having me locked up as a congenital lunatic? or both which she once seemed to think possible. Nevertheless we went to Folkestone for an interview.

The headmistress was Miss Gosling. She sat patiently behind her desk as Mummy held forth on the subject of education, brandishing the gloves clutched in her right hand and giving Miss Gosling the benefit of her superior knowledge.

When she paused for breath, Miss Gosling smiled graciously and said, 'Thank you, Mrs Innes. I'd like to speak to Elizabeth now, if I may.'

Mummy plonked the gloves onto her lap and stiffened her back.

Miss Gosling asked me questions about my interests, what I was good at, and what I'd like to do better. I sat up straight and used my best BBC pronunciation as instructed by Mummy. Finally Miss Gosling said, 'Tell me the most interesting thing you've learned lately.'

I told her about the machair of the Outer Hebrides.

'Machair,' she said, 'I haven't heard of that. How do you spell it?' She wrote it down and said, 'Well, Elizabeth, I think we will get along very well.' She held out her hand for me to shake.

I looked at Mummy but she had closed her face and I couldn't read her at all.

### *Upon my oath.*

The long summer holiday stretched ahead, with time to think about the future. But first there were places to go and people to see.

My mother had a friend and colleague called Valerie Kent who lived in Broadstairs, and contrived to have her babies in the summer holidays. She was warm and motherly. You could talk to her. I'd met her last year and could see she was expecting. I asked her how the baby got out and she said I didn't need to know that just yet, but it did hurt rather.

It couldn't hurt that much, I thought, as she was about to have another one, her fourth, and we were staying for a fortnight, to help with the other children, Tristram, Dolores and Louisa-Jane, all of them under school age. Before we went, Mummy asked me to make a promise. She took out her Bible.

'I'm going to tell you something very secret,' she said, 'but before I do you must swear before God that you will *never* talk about it to anyone else. Put your hand on the book.'

I repeated the oath after her and then she drew a picture, a cross-section of a cat. Inside it was a womb full of kittens. 'This,' she said with great gravity, 'is how babies grow.'

I knew that already. I'd known it since I was six. There were pictures in Daddy's books; women with upside-down babies inside.

Now I'd promised never to mention it. I was gagged. Why could I never ask anyone? Why was it so terrible? But I'd promised on the Bible, and God might strike me down if I said I already knew. I said nothing and my promise scared me half to death for years.

### *Family feeling.*

The Kents lived in an old cottage, up a lane off The Vale in Broadstairs. It had no electricity, though it did have gas, a water-tap in the kitchen, and a loo across the yard.

Also in residence was the Kents' friend, Rundle Brandon, a young poet, known as Bun, from a family of hoteliers in Bude who didn't know what to do with him. He wore corduroys and sandals and a forelock of curly hair that flopped over his eyes. We shared a room ... if you could call it that.

Half the cottage was derelict. There was a twisty stair with a door at the bottom and beyond the two main bedrooms, was a further room, which was minus much of its floor. Two rickety beds perched on planks. Bun's on the far side was reached by balancing on a joist. Mine was tucked just inside the door. I had charge of the candle in case it dropped through to the old stable below. By day I could see beneath us a heap of straw and a wrecked grand piano. At night little creatures rustled. It was exciting and I learned to be very careful with candles.

Valerie was an artist. There were dancing pixies and apple trees on the walls and fairies up the stairs. Her husband Geoffrey worked nights at the telephone exchange, and wrote children's stories by day, while Valerie taught at the school.

I loved being with the Kents. Every morning Tristram and Dolores piled into my bed with a couple of cats and snuggled about giggling until Valerie called us downstairs. After breakfast I was sent back to Margate on the bus to collect our mail from The Cecil. Afternoons we spent on the beach.

Broadstairs had rock-pools with crabs and shrimps, immovable limpets, and sea anemones like jewels. It was restful. I wondered if they could adopt me so that Mummy could be free of me. I could live forever in this wild melee of cats and kids and cooking where no one would mind if I was mad. But the new baby arrived and we returned to Margate. In days we were off to Clacton, and preparations for a wedding.

### *Hair*

Mummy's cousin Joyce was marrying her handsome airman. I needed a bridesmaid's dress. Skeena became the cradle of haute couture! There was snipping and stitching, and tacking and tucking and mouths full of pins!

Granny and Mummy were super-seamstresses. I learned a lot from them about fabrics and how they behave, how to alter patterns and place them for cutting, how to match cottons, to hem with not a stitch showing, and how to press a curved seam. They were in their element. They let me help and I almost felt I belonged

In the space of a few days they ran up all our wedding outfits, and some everyday clothes for my weekends at school, a dress and a tartan skirt. The skirt had shoulder straps, which slipped round the sides of my bust and made it more prominent. Embarrassing, said Granny. Disgusting, said Mummy. The straps were removed. I had a waist now. My skirts stayed up on their own.

I wasn't looking forward to the smell of Granny's Home Perm, but as usual the bowls and sachets and implements were laid out on the card table. Granny prepared herself, but first I needed my annual trim; hair tied back, half an inch off, and singed with a taper to stop split ends. I settled onto the chair. There was a tug and a crunch. Hair flopped over my face. Granny gasped.

'Win! What have you *done*?'

I leapt up and screamed. Mummy had my hair in her hand.

'I've brought another perm for you, Mother. This one's for Elizabeth.'

I was taller than Granny now but I wished I was half her height and could run to her skirt as I used to.

Granny said, 'Well, it can't be undone now, chicken. Have the perm. I'll make you look nice for the wedding.' and so she did, setting my hair with Amami lotion and pinning it back with combs and fabric butterflies. It looked very pretty but the fuss and bother put me off perms for life.

### *Other plans.*

I worried what Mummy's 'other plans' might be. Some sort of madhouse seemed likely. There had been no dancing, singing or acting for two years, so the 'child star' plan must be dead. Last time we saw Robert Donat I'd said I wanted to be a physicist. He sent Mummy a record; "Don't Put Your Daughter on the Stage, Mrs Worthington!" by Noel Coward.

'There you are! That's what Robert thinks of you!' said Mummy. She sang snatches.

*"The width of her seat would surely defeat*
*Her chances of success."*

Poor Robert! I think he was trying to help me. He was a gentleman and would never have been so hurtful, but I did see it as Mummy's view of me, and became very self-conscious. I had grown tall. The waist of my dress was up round my chest, and my feet were huge.

I needed shoes. UK size six. The woman in the shop measured my feet twice to be sure. Mummy sang,

*"Yo feet's too big. Ah duzzen luv ya coz yo feet's too big."*

'Oh Mummy don't!'

My mother's feet were a three and a half so mine must have looked quite gross to her. The shop assistant said, 'Mummy doesn't mean it. I'm sure she loves you very much.'

I forced a smile. I said, 'We can't all have little twinkle-toes like you, Mummy.'

Mummy beamed. 'I just wish we could do something about the smell.' she said. She was right.

'I don't mind.' I said, winding her up. 'They remind me of Daddy.' The expected slap didn't come. I felt smug.

I knew my school would be all girls and to be honest the boys had grown away from us somewhat. Not because they got more boyish, but because *we'd* changed. Suddenly we were taller than they, and stronger. I was taller than everyone, and felt like a hulking great lump.

There'd been little time to catch up with people at "Sunshine & Smiles" but at last I could tell Chuck and Billy about my exams.

'Boarding-school eh?' they said, 'They'll teach you to be a proper lady.'

'It's all girls,' I said, 'so I might not go. Mummy told Granny I might not be a woman. Some people change.'

'Course you are!' said Billy, 'Look at you! Whatever is she saying?'

Chuck said, 'There's a bloke in America got himself turned into a woman. Had an operation.' Billy winced.

Chuck said, 'She reads too many papers, your Mum.' but Billy said he hadn't seen it in the papers over here.

'It'll be all right.' I said, 'I know I'm a woman coz I ...' Oops! I felt my cheeks burn.

'Coz what?' said Chuck.

'coz ... I get let off doing gym.' I said, all of a rush.

'Oh THAT! ... and all that rubbish I expect about not washing your hair and going swimming. You should talk to the chorus about that. It's not as if the girls can take a week off every time. Talk to Babs Fox. She'll set you right.' I could have hugged him.

Babs Fox was head of chorus and hard to find, but I talked to Mandy's big sister, the one who'd identified the whiskers under my arms. It seemed that modern girls were not so delicate, so hair washing was fine, but swimming was a problem for other reasons. Meanwhile, as I was so grown up, I ought to try a cigarette. She gave me a Turf. It was disgusting.

### *Answering back*

The perm meanwhile had deteriorated. Perms had to be set and styled daily, and kept dry or they turned to a frizz. Mummy hacked some more off it, to make it tidy, she said.

'You can't go to a posh school like Folkestone with straight hair. You'll be a laughing stock.' she stood back. 'You look very smart.

'No I don't. I look like a ruddy hedgehog!

'*What* was that word?'

'Ruddy, Mummy. It means a reddish colour, though hedgehogs *are* a bit browner.

I felt pleased with myself for a while, but guilty later, I had wound Mummy up deliberately. I asked God to forgive me.

I could only see Mandy secretly now because she hadn't passed the exam. She was no longer suitable as a friend. I was angry. Mandy and Terry were the same people they were before the results. I shouted at my mother. I'd heard a few choice phrases in the cowboy films on Saturdays, though I'd never used one. I did now.

'Mandy? Common? Like *HELL* she is!'

I ran off to the beach fuming.

Margate had recovered well from the floods, though the shredded pier was a miserable sight. The air was evening-cool. I stood at the water's edge, daring the little waves to touch my sandals.

I'd done it again. I'd been rude to Mummy. Why was I being so ungrateful? Why couldn't I help myself? I wanted to be the perfect child, the perfect pupil. I wanted her to like me, but sometimes I just had to say what I thought.

Daddy would have understood. He'd have let me speak out, and told me quietly if I'd gone too far. Where was he? Did he know I'd got into Grammar School? There was no one I dared ask.

Never mind. There was a uniform to buy, name-tapes to sew, a cabin-trunk. Boarding School! I would learn Latin, and French. I'd sleep in a bed of my own.

I would miss Margate, though Folkestone wasn't too far away, and at least I'd come back in the holidays and see my friends, and the librarians, and the people at the café. "Sunshine and Smiles" would be gone, but Mummy would know where they were.

I remembered standing once on Clacton Pier, realizing that I needed to enjoy wherever I was and not miss the rest. What was it Daddy used to say?

*"The world is so full of a number of things.*
*I'm sure we should all be as happy as kings."*

That would depend on whether Kings were happy, of course. I'd have to think about that.

I had followed the receding tide as far as I dared. Now it had turned and reached my toes again. Shadows lengthened. Time to go home. Happily diverted by my new philosophical conundrum, I walked back to the Cecil Hotel.

***To be continued ...***

# *About the Author*

Liz Dyer was born in New Malden Surrey in 1942, but from six weeks old lived in Handsworth, Birmingham until she started school. She has lived in many places since then, most of them in childhood. She has been a folk singer, proprietor of a walkers' hostel, an office minion and a housewife. Although a life-long secret scribbler, her first published piece was a contribution to Lesley Close's 2014 book *"Assisted Dying: Who makes the final choice?"* She intends to write more volumes of memoir. Liz Dyer has lived in Derbyshire for almost thirty years. She still sings.

# *A work in progress*

**1954**

Mail was distributed at morning break. Weeks passed and there was nothing for me. Doc resorted to sarcasm. 'I suspect your mother has left the country.'

That might not be too bad, I thought. I could go to Granny in the holidays.

I had been six weeks at Horncastle when Doc handed me a fat envelope. 'Your mother's broken arm seems to have healed at last!' she said.

* * *

**1956**

My reaction to Suez and the Hungarian revolution was not so much fear as a terrible grief. Englishmen, Frenchmen, Jews and Egyptians, and most of all Hungarians. Every floating corpse in the Danube was someone with hopes come to nought. Perhaps it was my lack of proper bonds ... or maybe it's how you feel at fourteen.

Every human soul was potentially mine to love, and if I loved them enough they would love me back. Their mothers might be my mother and make me their family. Those families were out there now, bereft and afraid, so whatever side they were on every death was personal.

* * *

1958

'They 'as ter do it to yer once yer married, but if you really love 'im you won't mind ... an anyway ... 'e's goin' ta wrap you up in 'is arms and look after yer for ever an ever.'

Pam's assessment of conjugal duty was close to the accepted view ... and we were not to know the details until we married. We tried quizzing OT Deidre who was Irish and might be more forthcoming. 'Well, they say it's loik going to the dentist,' she said, 'Not pleasant but it has to be done.' She would say no more.

# *Acknowledgements*

I am grateful to the digital pioneers without whom etc; to those who, long ago, set up the internet, unaware of the paths it would open; to the countless writers who inhabit it; to the search engines who find me anything from a poet to a parliamentary debate.

I am grateful to Amazon KDP for opening the door to writers at every level, and whose detailed and thorough instructions taught me more about word-processing in thirty minutes than I learned in the previous thirty years.

And thanks go to Facebook, and the dozens of friends and relations who found me after years in limbo, read my contributions and encouraged me to write. Their comments and professional skills have ranged from confirmation of the side effects of bromide to a wide-ranging 'share' that identified my grandfather's Hudson Terraplane from a blurred headlamp and part of a radiator.

The Writing Group at Ashbourne U3A, have brought me encouragement and invaluable friendships over the last three years and helped me find my writer's voice. Special thanks go to Gina Harris, my beta reader, ever eager for the next installment.

Lastly I give thanks to the Derby Heritage Traditional Music Club, who dragged me from the shadows, made me sing again, and spent a decade restoring my confidence. Without that I would not be writing at all. And I give my love and thanks to Keith Kendrick and Sylvia Needham who listen to my ramblings and make sure I occasionally get out of the house.

*Liz Dyer*
*January 2019*

45984867R00139

Printed in Poland
by Amazon Fulfillment
Poland Sp. z o.o., Wrocław